Gambling With Your Soul

Gambling With Your Soul

What Is Your Best Bet?

Henry Arnold Davis

RESOURCE *Publications* · Eugene, Oregon

GAMBLING WITH YOUR SOUL
What Is Your Best Bet?

Resource Publications
An Imprint of Wipf and Stock Publishers
199 W. 8th Ave., Suite 3
Eugene, OR 97401

www.wipfandstock.com

PAPERBACK ISBN: 978-1-6667-0183-8
HARDCOVER ISBN: 978-1-6667-0184-5
EBOOK ISBN: 978-1-6667-0185-2

05/13/21

Dedicated to Eddie Lee Davis—Dee La,
whose quiet strength, compassion, and determination
fueled my passion for knowledge.

Contents

List of Illustrations and Tables

Acknowledgments

To MY SWEET WIFE and lifelong partner, Tanya, for her patience and unwavering support during the writing of this book, which increased the demands on our family and rivaled the amount of time it takes most university professors to get tenure. Thanks for embarking on this journey with me and your tireless efforts, thoughtful edits, and well-timed, "How's it going?" which were confirmations to stay the course.

To my little brother and spiritual compass, Marvin Davis, with a heart the size of Texas, a discerning eye, and an unconditional love for humanity. Thank you for giving the book its heart and soul.

To my big brother and confidant, Ran Davis, who provided invaluable feedback on a very early and extremely rough draft of the manuscript—if you could call it that. Thanks for your keen insight which helped crystallize the book's focus.

To my patient and determined big brother, Vernon Davis, who provided irreplaceable details to an all but "finished" manuscript. Thanks for your persistence, which rounded out some critical content.

To my big sister, author, and songwriter, Joyce Tines, who connected the dots and provided the right perspective to weave some vital strands together. Thanks for your fine-tuning and allowing the book to stay true to its intent.

To my sister-in-law and legal eagle, Penny Davis, who helped clear the last hurdle in getting the book to the finish line. Thanks for applying your sharp analytical skills and trained eyes in making sure all i's were dotted and t's crossed to let the work soar to new heights.

To my friend, fellow Bulldog, and writing mentor, Christina Baker Kline, whose warm spirit creates a welcoming embrace for all in its presence. Thanks for your gentle yet firm guiding hand that kept the project on the straight and narrow—always moving forward.

Acknowledgments

To my friend, fellow Snake, and creative inspiration, Sylvia Brown-rigg, who helped expand the team's support structure in ways that cannot be measured. Thanks for your incredible resourcefulness, which helped the project overcome any obstacle that bubbled to the surface.

To my friend and fellow Davenporter, Gardiner Harris, who set the project on a solid foundation with straightforward and effective know-how. Thanks for being the springboard that pushed the needle in the right direction.

To my friend and former crewmate, Ramsey Walker, whose generosity is without end. Thanks for being the coxswain who navigated the deep waters and helped steer this boat safely to its ultimate destination.

To my friend, former business partner, and fellow board member, Micheal R. Watkins Sr., who became a sounding board for all the ideas and directions explored in the early development of the research, materials, and messages that filled the funnel. Thank you for sharing your wisdom.

To my editor, Lisa Webster, whose pen is most definitely mightier than the sword. Thanks for your sage advice and relentless pursuit of perfection in driving this work to be the best it could be.

To my friend and former business partner, James Austin Whittaker, who was able to see the big picture as well as the finite detail. Thank you for providing the perfect balance of critique and criticism to ensure ideas were fully vetted.

To my friend, former roommate, and tennis aficionado, Tim Willke, who I've always counted on to tell it like it is. Thanks for challenging some key assumptions and providing a refreshing viewpoint that will undoubtedly broaden the book's reach.

To the many relatives, friends, colleagues,
classmates, acquaintances, and strangers
from around the globe,
who indulged my curiosity while traveling
through the air, over land, or on the water, having a meal,
enjoying a beverage, or taking a stroll in a park,
along the beach, across campus, or down Main Street.
Thank you for sharing your thoughts, questions, and stories
—the oxygen that ignited the spark which set this work on fire.

Introduction

EVERY PILOT, WHETHER IT'S their first solo or the one thousandth time braving the wild blue yonder, will tell you that one of the most important aspects of air travel is preflight planning. A disciplined preflight planning regiment—often captured in a checklist by a team of experienced airmen/women, aircraft mechanics, safety officers, quality personnel, and other support staff—can be the difference between a successful journey, and one filled with issues and regrets.

Preflight planning looks at all the significant variables a pilot could encounter in getting from point A to point B. It addresses questions like: What type of weather can be expected? What will be the terrain and geographical features below—water, mountains, ice, forest, desert, etc.? At what altitudes will the aircraft need to fly and for what distances? Will the trip involve flying at night when visibility is reduced? Will the pilot be flying under Instrument Flight Rules (IFR) or Visual Flight Rules (VFR)? Are there checkpoints along the way? How will the pilot communicate with air traffic control, various ground personnel, or other aircraft encountered during the flight? What kind of equipment will be needed? Supplies? How much equipment and supplies will be needed? Is the crew all present and accounted for? And probably most important, what is the condition of the aircraft?

Proven to be an effective process—battle tested by thousands of pilots across the globe over many years, this routine only works if the pilot knows where he is going. In Stephen R. Covey's *The 7 Habits of Highly Effective People*, this is identified as habit #2—Begin with the End in Mind. It's based on principles of personal leadership and found in many people's daily activities. This habit is also regarded as the second most important behavior exhibited by individuals who routinely deliver successful results.

Architects plan, design, and review the construction of a building before the first nail is hammered. The coach draws up the perfect play long before the players execute it. Engineers can go through eight design revisions before any raw material is ordered. To build that masterpiece envisioned in their mind's eye, they shoot for perfection. And the soccer mom plans her day in advance to arrive at her son's piano recital, her daughter's lacrosse game, and her spouse's work function on time. She's also dressed in the appropriate attire for each event—bringing along the right backup gear. Just in case the weather doesn't align with the forecast, which of course won't be needed. The weather forecast is never wrong.

Without a specific endpoint—in virtually all endeavors, but especially with air travel—the variables analyzed could yield very different results. This could lead to decisions and actions with unintended and undesirable consequences. Imagine checking the weather forecast in the dead of winter between Chicago and Atlanta, and then flying from Chicago to Boston. Or having enough fuel to fly from Los Angeles to Denver, but going—or more accurately, trying to go—from LA to Detroit instead. How about calculating weight and balance based on twelve passengers, but twenty-four people and eight animals show up to board the aircraft.

Now—as we learned in grade school—the shortest distance between two points is a straight line. But the pilot can still get from point A to point B without traveling in a straight line. Depending on the circumstances encountered during the flight, the best route may not be straight. It might be a zigzag, a step-up-n-down, a loop-d-loop, or a type of line the world has not yet defined.

The pilot may not be able to anticipate every situation he could encounter on the journey. He might need to improvise along the way. Maybe take a few unplanned detours or make some midcourse corrections. And that's alright. So long as he keeps his eyes focused on the forest and not the trees, he will continue moving away from point A and closer to point B. The pilot, crew, and passengers may arrive a bit late, but they all get to their intended destination safely. And at the end of the day, that's what really matters.

In the case of our journey through life, from birth to the grave and possibly beyond, isn't that also what really matters—that we arrive safely at our intended destination? But you might ask, what is our destination? Is it the same place for every person? Are there specific destinations for certain groups of people? Or does each of us have our own unique destination we are trying to reach? Taking the advice of Stephen R. Covey, we return to habit #2. Regardless of the answer to these questions, if we want to improve the odds of achieving our goal—arriving safely at our destination—we must first begin with the end in mind. And this leads us to perhaps an even larger and more fundamental question.

What is "The End" for a human being?

1

Death Walks In

When the Lamb opened the fourth seal, I heard the voice of the fourth living
creature say, "Come!" I looked, and there before me was a pale horse! Its rider
was named Death, and Hades was following close behind him.

—REVELATION 6:7–8 NIV

But rather than be sad, wouldn't it be a lot better to face our own death
knowing that our life had been lived to the fullest and without regret?
Even though we may not want to face death, it is inevitable
just as it is for the setting sun each evening.

—BYRON PULSIFER

The boundaries which divide Life from Death are at best shadowy and vague.
Who shall say where the one ends, and where the other begins?

—EDGAR ALLAN POE

Kapow! THE UNMISTAKABLE SOUND of a gunshot shatters the night silence
as the gunman forces his way into the locked apartment. Lacking a key, he
resorted to fire power.

The apartment is well lit and airy, featuring an open floor plan. It has
two levels with high ceilings and stairs off the main entrance. Furniture is

arranged comfortably within the rooms. The artwork and greenery add just the right accents, but he pays no attention to these details.

His heart rate is accelerated, and his palms are sweaty. Shouting out the owner's name, he realizes she is not there. As he rushes throughout the living space, his eyes scan each room in an instant. No signs of the occupant.

Spotting an open window, he races to it and hears hurried footsteps from above. The cool night breeze feels good on his face. But no time to enjoy that.

The apartment owner, Molly, and another woman are racing up a flight of metal fire escape stairs. Each step echoes as if they are in Laurel Caverns—the deepest cave in the northeastern United States.[1] The women are heading to a vacant penthouse apartment to elude their assailant.

The scaffolding, paint buckets, plastic, and construction tools testify to ongoing renovations. The wind catches the plastic and whips it back and forth like a flag atop Mount Everest—the windiest place on earth.[2] The women crawl through an open window, pausing momentarily to close it behind them—as if this will stop the gunman from pursuing them. On second thought, they decide he's too close to risk being caught. Better keep moving.

They stumble into the room exhausted from the quick climb and continuously pleading with the gunman. "Leave us alone, Carl! I've already called the police," Molly yells. She is nearly out of breath.

Carl knows the women and doesn't want to hurt them. But he will if they do not give him what he wants.

The women elude him by climbing up a ladder onto the scaffolding and pulling the ladder up. They scamper along the scaffolding's work platform—three eight-inch wooden planks laid side by side and end to end—running throughout the room like an intricately designed maze. Ten feet above the room's floor, they are safely out of their assailant's reach.

Desperate to catch them—and without the benefit of a ladder, Carl surveys the room for another way to close the gap between his six-foot-two-inch frame and the scaffolding's work platform. He spots a nearby table. It's just ahead of the women and in line with their projected escape route. "Perfect," he says to himself. Not out loud. "I can reach them by standing on it."

1. *Wikipedia*, s.v. "Laurel Caverns."
2. Wallner, "7 Windiest Places."

He sprints to the table and with a powerful, athletic move jumps on top of it—arriving just as the last woman is crossing over his head. He has a brief flashback to his high school glory days as a track star. High hurdles. Man, he misses those days. He wonders to himself, "How did I end up here?" Carl shoves those thoughts back into the crevices of his mind, reaches up, grabs the leg of the older woman, and pulls her down.

Oda Mae crashes onto the table then falls to the ground. At gunpoint, he demands that she hand over the check, but Oda Mae no longer has it. "Don't lie to me!" Carl shouts. Sticking the gun into her face, he has no choice. He prepares to fire his weapon, when suddenly he is shoved violently.

Seething with anger, Carl fires into the dark room. He is unable to see who or what has pushed him, but he already knows. A similar thing had happened in a previous encounter.

The women are being protected by a ghost, who has stepped in to fight the gunman on their behalf.

During the ensuing battle, Carl finds himself leaning backward in the open window through which he entered the apartment. He discovers an overhead chain with a large hook. He swings it at the ghost. The chain, of course, has no impact on the ghost; and like a pendulum, swings back toward Carl. It strikes the windowpane above him and shatters it. The window-dowpane is reduced to a jagged 24 by 36-inch piece of glass with a knife-like point. The window free falls eight feet with a sound like someone dragging their fingernails across a chalkboard. The glass lodges in his chest, killing him instantly.

Carl's soul separates from his body but doesn't realize what has happened. He thinks he is still alive and is obviously in a very confused state. He is now able to see the ghost with whom he has been fighting. It is his friend, Sam.

Sam was murdered by a man hired by Carl. The man was not supposed to kill him, but things had gone bad. Very bad.

As Carl tries to wrap his mind around this new reality, Sam looks past Carl's soul back at the body laying slumped in the open window. A hunk of glass sticking out of its chest. Carl follows Sam's eyes and turns around to see what's behind him.

Then slowly, complete with blood-curdling sounds—the kind that make the hair on the back of your neck stand up—dark, grotesque figures emerge from the floor. They grab ahold of Carl's soul. His soul struggles mightily. But it's hopeless. With shrieks of agony, Carl's soul is dragged kicking and screaming down below and fades out of sight.

The two women, now safe from harm, are found huddled together in a corner of the room. Sam asks them if they are alright. To her amazement, Molly can now hear him.

Before Sam's death, he and Molly had moved in together, with plans to be married. They had also been friends with Carl. Or at least they thought so. Sam and Carl had worked together, but something had gone wrong with a financial deal. To rectify the situation, Carl needed information which only Sam had. He hired someone to mug Sam and steal his wallet, which contained the information. However, the mugging did not go as planned, and the mugging turned into murder.

Then surprisingly both women see Sam. He is illuminated by a bright light from above. In fact, there are many small lights twinkling and glowing—most likely symbolic of individual souls or spirits.

The older woman, Oda Mae Brown, has been gifted with the ability to communicate with the dead. She tells Sam it is time for him to leave this earth and join the bright lights waiting for him. It is evident that Sam, when he was alive, was a good person. Therefore, his reward in the afterlife is going to a place of goodness and peace.

As he says goodbye to the women and to this world, Sam tells them that the love he had while alive is still with him as he enters the next life. The scene ends with Sam walking toward a brilliant array of blinding lights while soft, peaceful music plays in the background. Not a dry eye on the screen or in the theater.

Anticipation

That was the final scene from the 1990 American blockbuster *Ghost*. It's one of my favorite Hollywood movies. Is this art imitating life, or will life imitate art?

The film industry has tackled some of the most profound questions facing society. It all started in Richmond, Indiana, in June 1894. Charles Francis Jenkins used his Phantoscope to project his film onto the silver screen. He unveiled his creation before an audience of his family, friends, and reporters. Today the film industry is approaching a trillion dollars with the world's two most populous countries leading the way. According to

Statista Research & Analysis, China generates the most revenue from box offices. And India produces the most films.

Research by psychologists has shown that movies can influence our attitudes and behavior. Clinical psychologist, psychotherapist, research scientist, and emeritus professor of psychology Dr. Victor B. Cline—cofounder of the organization Marriage and Family Enrichment—acknowledged, "There appears to be little doubt that television and motion pictures have significant power to inform, educate, persuade, and sometimes even change behavior." And while there is a recent trend to base films on real-life events, most movies are fictional.

I suppose I want to believe that if I live a good life, whatever that means, then I will be rewarded with a good afterlife—if there is such a thing. Also, with my sense of fair play, I would expect some sort of punishment in the afterlife if I had done bad or evil things while alive. Of course, it depends on what is considered bad or evil. We'll come back to that later.

For now, the million-dollar question is, "Can humans expect what is depicted in the blockbuster movie when they die?" Now, this general question is undoubtedly of interest—on an intellectual or philosophical level. But let's be honest. The question you and I are most interested in answering—on a deeply personal level—is specifically, "What will happen to me when I die?" That is "The Question."

The Question has confounded mankind from the moment intelligent thought was born. Ecclesiastes 7:4 (New Living Translation) states that "a wise person thinks a lot about death, while a fool thinks only about having a good time." At some point in our lives, we have all probably asked ourselves—at least once—The Question. For me, it first occurred at eight years of age. I was sitting on a sofa in the living room of our eight-hundred-square-foot house in Memphis.

A Nightmare on Hazelwood Road

At 1:00 a.m. on a school night, it was well past my bedtime. Ordinarily I would have been entering my second REM sleep cycle. But this was no ordinary night.

On the sofa, I was joined by my two younger brothers, Marvin and Allen. We were in our pajamas trying desperately to keep our eyes open. Exactly why we were there had been lost to us. We were now focused on the revolver under a white-knuckled death grip in our father's hand.

Dad leaned forward in the chair across from the sofa. The veins in his face bulging from his temples. One of us boys had done something to upset our dad—to really upset him—and we were not telling him the truth. "If one of you don't tell me the truth, I'm going to kill all of you," Dad threatened. "Sis (that was his nickname for our mother), you know I'll do it. I'll start with the oldest"—raising the gun, almost in slow motion, and pointing it at me, then, letting his stare and the weapon's hollow opening stay fixated long enough to have the intended effect—"and won't stop until the youngest."

Mom was sitting in the only other chair in the cramped living room, shaking uncontrollably with tears welling in her eyes. Between sobs, she was pleading with our dad—David, that's what she called him, although his given name was James—to calm down. To this day, I don't completely understand why she called him David. I once asked her about it. She simply replied, "Your father awoke one morning and demanded, 'Don't call me James anymore. I'm tired of that name.' And that was that."

My father had a hauntingly stern voice that could put the fear of God in you without laying a finger on you. And it was being wielded that night with precision—stabbing me in the heart with every other word. The tension in the room was thick enough to cut with a knife. I was scared. Beyond scared. But I had somehow found a way to stay reasonably calm.

The surreal scene had gone on for several hours, and this was not the first night it had been played out. Would this be the night with a different ending? I tried to remember exactly how many times it had happened but had lost count. My dad had a problem controlling his anger. He could go from being the nicest person in the world to a fire-breathing dragon in the blink of an eye. And while this was a much-too-frequent scene in my childhood, the current situation was very much real. It could have surely led to my death as my father was threatening.

He may have even felt justified in doing it. My older brothers and sisters would tell us smaller kids—the youngest eight or so out of seventeen— that Dad used to be worse. Much worse.

Several years earlier, the abuse had become so severe my older siblings had to bring it to an end by any means necessary. They meticulously planned every detail of the operation, including who would pull the trigger. The plan would be carried out in the early morning hours while Dad slept on the pullout sofa in the living room. A single shot strategically placed would stop their pain and suffering.

While they thought their plan was flawless, there were some hidden factors—not surprisingly—they didn't account for.

It was a rainy night. There was nothing unusual about it. In our two-bedroom house, the boys had one bedroom and the girls shared the other. Mom and Dad normally slept together on the pullout sofa in the living room but not always. Also, on occasion, a baby slept with them. What if Dad was not sleeping in his normal spot—the left side of the bed? What if he wasn't asleep at all? What if the bullet missed Dad and hit Mom instead? What if it hit both Mom and Dad? What would happen if the gun misfired?

And if those weren't enough variables, my ten-year-old brother had never held a gun, much less fired one. But he was not deterred. This had to be done—no ifs, ands, or buts. He pushed all those questions, variables, and unknowns out of his young mind. Focused. Pointed the gun. And pulled the trigger. The fire from the barrel lit up the room like the first rays of sunrise above a dark horizon. Within the small house, the sound was deafening.

The 38-caliber bullet entered the right side of my father's chest—not the intended target. It rattled around in his thoracic cavity and exited between the sixth and seventh ribs just below his right arm pit. He survived—not my brother's intended outcome.

Dad never pressed charges against any of his children involved in the shooting. But I don't think he ever forgot or forgave them. In the days that followed the incident, there were obvious changes in the Davis household. I was too young to fully understand all the dynamics. Even so, it was clear Dad had become less involved in the children's discipline. I would discover years later this was due to an agreement he signed with the Tennessee Department of Human Services (DHS). He became withdrawn and distant. Almost nothing made him lose his temper, but the anger was still there, stewing. Maybe even more so than in the past, because now he had no release for it.

In the years that followed, the anger would slowly resurface. Bringing with it mental, physical, and emotional abuse until it became a full-blown rage at the slightest infraction that did not meet with his approval. Us younger children had been experiencing it now for the past few years. His agreement with DHS had long been forgotten.

Perhaps Dad would get revenge on his three youngest children for the wrong done to him by his older children—his own brand of poetic justice. Whatever his reasons could have been, at that moment in our living room, I just knew this time I was really going to die. I had accepted it in my eight-year-old mind as a foregone conclusion. So, sitting on that sofa in the wee hours of the morning, I found myself wondering, "What will happen to me when I die?"

In Search Of

My mother was a Christian and had taught me about Jesus Christ and heaven and hell. My dad also believed in heaven and hell but was not a Christian. He believed Jesus Christ was the illegitimate son of a Roman soldier. The church promoted him as a vehicle to, presumably, trick people into giving it all their money.

Well of course I did not die that night. Eventually, Dad calmed down and allowed us kids to go to bed. The next morning when we awoke for school, there was no discussion about the night before. Unfortunately, scenes like that one had become all too common in our young lives. Walking home—the last place on earth we wanted to be—from school that afternoon, Marvin and I talked. Our hope and prayers were to live at least to age eighteen so we could get out of the house—for good.

We did grow up and moved on with our lives. However, it was those childhood experiences that prompted me to seriously wrestle with The Question. Once I accepted the fact that one day I was going to die, it was a natural next thought. Therefore, I have thought about it on more than one occasion.

During those occasions, I have presented, discussed, debated, and downright argued The Question with many people—representing thirty-five countries and territories on every continent except Antarctica. As you can probably imagine, I have received countless different answers. On one end of the spectrum, respondents claimed that absolutely nothing at all happens. When you die, you die. That's it. It's over. At the other end, individuals were convinced that everyone goes to a place of their choosing and does whatever they want to do. Some people took the position that they don't know what happens, and they don't care to think about it.

So, what is the answer?

Reflections

What movies, books, people, events, or experiences have shaped your beliefs about the afterlife?

When was the last time you thought about death?

Are you prepared to die?

2

Being Human

Mistakes are a part of being human. Appreciate your mistakes
for what they are: precious life lessons that can only be learned the hard way.
Unless it's a fatal mistake, which, at least, others can learn from.

—AL FRANKEN

If you don't have imagination, you stop being human; animals don't have
imagination; Alzheimer's is the death of imagination.

—DEVDUTT PATTANAIK

Challenging the meaning of life is the truest expression
of the state of being human.

—VIKTOR E. FRANKL

WHAT DOES HAPPEN TO human beings when they die? Well, before we can
answer that question, we need to ask a more basic question. What is a human being? And more specifically, what are you?

Making Me, Me

If this seems like an odd question, you are not alone. That's probably because we are not presented with it in our normal course of daily living. The typical phrasing would be *who are you* as opposed to *what are you.*

If you were being interviewed for a job, you would likely start by telling where you went to school, in which branch of the military you served, or the jobs you've held. You may talk about some of your accomplishments. You would elaborate on your strengths, being sure to cover both the hard and soft skills that make you an ideal candidate for the job. If you are feeling brave or comfortable, you may even dive—not too deep—into some of your "personal" life. Commenting on your marital status and the number of kids or perhaps grandkids you have. Maybe you share that you are an only child or the fifteenth of seventeen children in my case. You might wrap up by touching on some of your hobbies and what you enjoy doing outside of work. The intent is to show that you are a well-rounded individual and a good fit for their culture.

But would this be a suitable explanation to tell someone who or what you are? Or is it rather an explanation of what you do, have done, or enjoy doing? Our experiences are certainly key ingredients in shaping our beliefs and perceptions of ourselves. However, they do not actually explain what we are. That was decided long before we began to have any experiences, make a single decision, or take any actions at all.

In the Beginning

Pro-Life advocates argue that a human life begins at conception, when a male sperm fertilizes or unites with a female egg (oocyte). Some even propose that the actual male sperm and female oocyte represent human life even before they come together during fertilization to form a zygote.

Dr. Jerome Lejeune, an accomplished physician, scientist and winner of the William Allen Memorial Award, the world's highest honor in genetics, once stated that "To accept the fact that after fertilization has taken place a new human has come into being is no longer a matter of taste or opinion . . . it is plain experimental evidence." In *[The] Basics of Biology* [by Carol Leth Stone] five characteristics of living things are given. These five criteria are found in all modern elementary scientific textbooks:

1. Living things are highly organized.

2. All living things have an ability to acquire materials and energy.

3. All living things have an ability to respond to their environment.

4. All living things have an ability to reproduce.

5. All living things have an ability to adapt.

According to this elementary definition of life, life begins at fertilization, when a sperm unites with an oocyte. From this moment, the being is highly organized. It can acquire materials and energy, respond to his or her environment, is able to adapt, and capable of reproducing (the cells divide, then divide again, etc., and barring pathology and pending reproductive maturity has the potential to reproduce other members of the species). Non-living things do not do this.

Even before the mother is aware that she is pregnant, a distinct, unique life has begun his or her existence inside her. Dr. Hymie Gordon—Chairman [of the] Department of Genetics at the Mayo Clinic, asserts that "By all the criteria of modern molecular biology, life is present from the moment of conception."

Pro-Choice proponents on the other hand contend that there is no scientific consensus of exactly when life begins for a human being. Biologist Scott Gilbert, an expert in human development, tells us that there are at least four distinct moments that can be thought of as the beginning of human life. Each can be said to be biologically accurate.

1. The genetic view (the position held by the Roman Catholic Church and many religious conservatives) holds that life begins with the acquisition of a novel genome; it is a kind of genetic determinism.

2. Those who hold the embryologic view think life begins when the embryo undergoes gastrulation, and twinning is no longer possible; this occurs about 14 days into development. (Some mainline Protestant religions espouse a similar view.)

3. Proponents of the neurological view adhere to brainwave criteria; life begins when a distinct EEG pattern can be detected, about 24 to 27 weeks. (Some Protestant churches affirm this.) Interestingly, life is also thought to end when the EEG pattern is no longer present.

4. Finally, one can say that life begins at or near birth, measured by fetal viability outside the mother's body. (Judaism affirms something close to this position.) After all, somewhere between 50 and 60 percent of all embryos conceived miscarry.[1]

The debate over the exact moment human life begins is certain to continue. Nevertheless, I am confident everyone can agree that it starts sometime between conception and nine months later. That's the approximate length of a full-term pregnancy. Now we know that some pregnancies may terminate sooner. The pregnancy could end by forced inducement or the baby simply announcing, "I'm coming out, ready or not." At that time, the fetus leaves the mother's body and enters our physical world. So, by the time a child enters the world, life has most definitely begun. And it is clearly a human being—to which there is no disagreement.

The child has not gone to school, enlisted in the military, or held down a job. She has not gotten married. There are no children of her own she can present. And she hasn't done anything that would allow her to talk about strengths and capabilities—although surviving nine months in a dark, tight space curled up inside another living organism is quite an accomplishment by itself. Now aside from being her parents' daughter, who is she? Or more appropriately, what is she?

The Three Musketeers

Of an estimated 8.7 million species that live on the planet,[2] human beings are members of the *Homo sapiens*—Latin for "wise man"—species. It is widely accepted that humans are composed of three interrelated yet separate components: the body, the mind, and the soul (sometimes referred to as the spirit, energy, or vital force within a person). This precise characterization is found primarily in Western and European civilizations. However, the underlying concept is virtually universal.

In many Eastern civilizations, where Yoga philosophy—one of the six major orthodox schools of Hinduism—is more prevalent, humans are thought to have three bodies: the physical, the subtle, and the super-subtle. The physical body is the same as the Western and European body. The subtle body is analogous to the mind, and the super-subtle body equates to

---

1. "When Does Life Begin?," http://www.familydoctormag.com/sexual-health/251-when-does-life-begin-medical-experts-debate-abortion-issue.html.

2. Camps, "How Many Species."

the soul or spirit. In certain parts of the world, including Africa, Asia, Australia, and Latin America, humans can have more than one soul or spirit.
For instance,

> Multiple souls, [is a] widely distributed notion, especially in central and northern Asia and Indonesia, that an individual's life and personality are made up of a complex set of psychic interrelations. In some traditions the various souls are identified with the separate organs of the body; in others they are related to character traits. Each of the different souls making up a single individual has a different destiny after death. Among many northern Asian peoples, for example, one soul remains with the corpse, one soul descends to the underworld, and one soul ascends to the heavens.
>
> The most famous example of multiple souls is the belief of the Apapocuva Guaraní of Brazil that a gentle vegetable soul comes, fully formed, from the dwelling place of the gods and joins with the infant at the moment of birth. To this is joined, shortly after birth, a vigorous animal soul. The type of animal decisively influences the recipient's personality: a gentle person has received a butterfly's soul; a cruel and violent man, the soul of a jaguar. Upon death, the vegetable soul enters paradise, and the animal soul becomes a fierce ghost that plagues the tribe.[3]

In other theologies such as Shinto—the ethnic religion of Japan—a human being does not have a unique soul or spirit. Shinto was Japan's state religion until 1945 and has no concept of an eternal human soul or spirit. Humans contain a portion of the universal and eternal spiritual energy known as kami. The religion teaches that upon death, the person's spiritual energy rejoins with kami. Kami is the spiritual energy that resides in all living, and in some cases, nonliving things. It is simply transferred or shifted from one entity to another. This philosophy aligns with the concept of energy conservation. The first law of thermodynamics—a version of the law of conservation of energy—states that heat energy can neither be created nor destroyed. It supports the assertion that energy can only be transferred or changed from one form to another.

Therefore, in essentially all the world's civilizations and known primal regions, a human being is believed to have at least one soul or spirit. This does include the concepts of a spiritual energy or vital force. Additionally, the being has a mind, along with a physical body. When a baby emerges

---

3. *Britannica.com*, s.v. "Multiple Souls."

from its mother's womb—or possibly some other surrogate incubation chamber—it is complete with all three components. The newborn is most assuredly a human being.

Reflections

What does being human mean to you?

When did life begin for you?

What makes you, you?

3

After The Life Is Gone

A beautiful body perishes, but a work of art dies not.
—LEONARDO DA VINCI

It is the mark of an educated mind to be able to
entertain a thought without accepting it.
—ARISTOTLE

You have to grow from the inside out. None can teach you,
none can make you spiritual. There is no other teacher but your own soul.
—SWAMI VIVEKANANDA

Now that we have determined what makes up a human being, let's get back to the question of what happens to us when we die. We now realize that the question must be answered for each of the three human components: the body, the mind, and the soul. Let's begin with the body—the physical body.

Hard Bodies

One of the most common fates of the physical body after a person's death is to be placed inside a coffin or casket. The coffin is then buried in the earth, usually six feet below the surface. Another form of burial in the earth is called natural or "green" burial. Here the body is placed in the soil without the protection of a coffin or casket. This method of burial was made popular in the United Kingdom in the early 1990s by Ken West—a professional crematory operator for the city of Carlisle and author of *A Guide to Natural Burial*. It has since spread to other countries, including Australia, Canada, Ireland, and the United States.[1]

Another popular choice is for the body to be wrapped in a cloth or other material, known as a shroud, and placed inside a tomb. The tomb can be either above or below ground. This was the most prevalent form of burial in ancient Israel during the time of Jesus Christ. It remains the most customary form of burial in the Middle East, as well as other places in the world. Other above ground rituals, such as sky burials in Tibet, leaves the body exposed to the elements or as food for animals.

Recently, more people have chosen to have their bodies cremated. And according to *Wikipedia*, it is the norm in India and mandatory in most parts of Japan.

Finally, there are those unfortunate instances where the deceased person's body is destroyed. This could be the result of a war or some other situation.

If not cremated, consumed by animals, or physically destroyed, medical science—and indeed actual observation—has shown that after death the human body decays over time. Leaving only the bones and teeth in the end. Now there are special chemicals used in the embalming process that can delay the body's decomposition. And certain processes, whether accidental or intentional, like mummification or cryonics, can slow or even stop the body from decomposing. With the rate of advancements in science and technology—heading toward a technological singularity, extropians are optimistic these practices will someday—in the not-too-distant future—bear fruit. However, thus far, no body that has been mummified or preserved through cryonics has ever been brought back to life.

Therefore, we can conclude that once a human being dies, the physical body also dies. And in most cases, it is destroyed. If not cremated, it will either decay, be consumed as food by animals, or in a few instances stay in a preserved state.

---

1. *Wikipedia*, s.v. "Burial."

Mind Over Matter

The next component of a human being is the mind or subtle body in Eastern civilizations. The United Negro College Fund reminds us that "a mind is a terrible thing to waste."

Throughout history some of the most intelligent humans to walk the planet have studied the mind. Important philosophers of mind include Plato, Patanjali, René Descartes, Gottfried Wilhelm Leibniz, John Locke, George Berkeley—known as Bishop Berkeley (Bishop of Cloyne)—David Hume, Immanuel Kant, G. W. F. Hegel, Arthur Schopenhauer, John Searle, Daniel Dennett, Jerry Fodor, Thomas Nagel, and David Chalmers. The description and definition of mind is also a part of psychology. Esteemed psychologists Sigmund Freud and William James have developed influential theories about the nature of the mind. And renowned computer scientists have also studied the mind. Alan Mathison Turing and Hilary Whitehall Putnam devoted significant time to develop impactful theories about the mind's makeup and operation.[2] Yet the mind remains one of the greatest mysteries of a human being.

One of the most difficult concepts to explain is the basic connection and interdependence of the physical brain and the mind. It's known as the mind-body problem.

Philosophy of mind is a branch of philosophy that studies the nature of the mind. It looks at the mind's mental events, mental functions, mental properties, and consciousness. It then considers their relationship to the physical body, particularly the brain. Dualism and monism are the two major schools of thought that attempt to resolve the mind-body problem.

Dualism can be traced back to the Sankhya and Yoga schools of Hindu philosophy and to Plato. It was also formulated by René Descartes in the seventeenth century.[3]

Dualism is the concept that the mind and the body, specifically the brain, are two distinct and separate things. They have a material and a nonmaterial component. The brain is the physical or material substance that can be touched, measured, weighed, and viewed with the naked eye. It is governed by the physics and mathematics within our universe and impacted by its natural laws and forces. All dualists accept this narrative of the

2. *Wikipedia*, s.v. "Mind."
3. *Wikipedia*, s.v. "Philosophy of Mind."

brain. The mind, however, is divided between two groups: substance and property dualists.

Substance dualists argue that the mind is an independently existing substance of a nonmaterial nature. It has a spiritual dimension that includes consciousness and the basis for thoughts, memories, the ability to reason, and the like. It is not subjected to the physical laws of our universe. You cannot touch it, measure it, weigh it, or see it.

Property dualists maintain that the mind is a group of independent nonphysical mental properties. These properties emerge from the brain but cannot be reduced to the brain. The mind is not a distinct substance. However, the mental properties (such as beliefs, desires, and emotions) attributable to the mind would be essentially the same as those advocated by substance dualists.

Therefore, for both substance and property dualists, the mind is separate from the physical brain. The mind manifests itself through the brain in a similar way sound waves manifest themselves through a radio. We enjoy the melodies being projected by the radio, but the music is not part of the radio.

Monism is the concept that the mind and body are not ontologically distinct kinds of entities. They are not independent substances. This view was first introduced in Western philosophy by Parmenides in the fifth century BC. Years later, it was espoused by the seventeenth-century rationalist Baruch Spinoza.[4]

Proponents of monism fall into two groups. They are identified as either physicalists (also referred to as materialists) or idealists. There are also subcategorizations within each group.

Physicalists argue that everything—including the human mind—in our universe is made of physical materials. They believe that any nonmaterial substances—if any exist—can be explained by a physical entity. If not completely by a physical entity, then through a dependence on a set of physical attributes.

Idealists maintain that the mind is all that exists. They claim that the external physical world is either mental itself, or an illusion created by the mind.

From either a physicalists or idealist perspective, the mind and brain are considered one and the same. Be it physical or mental. There is only one entity.

---

4. *Wikipedia*, s.v. "Mind-Body Perspectives."

Most modern philosophers of mind (including Jerry Fodor, Daniel Dennett, and Hilary Putnam) maintain, albeit in different ways, that the mind is not something separate from the body.[5] This is in line with the position advanced by monism, both physicalists and idealists.

So, the question to answer is, at the time of physical death and when the body is destroyed, what happens to the mind?

According to a physicalist (monism), the mind is also destroyed, since it is made of physical materials or exists wholly through its dependence on the physical body.

Idealists (monism) would argue that the mind continues after the body is destroyed, because the physical world does not actually exist anyway. The mind is the only thing that's real.

Proponents of dualism may not be as bold in their claim as idealists regarding the mind's survival after the destruction of the physical body. However, since dualists believe the mind and body are separate entities, they could reason that the mind can survive without a human body.

I should point out that the word mind is often used interchangeably with the words spirit or soul by dualists and idealists. Thus, when discussing the three components (body, mind, and soul) of a human being, mind and soul are sometimes lumped together, giving a human being only two components. In this makeup of a human being, there is agreement that the mind/soul/spirit survives the physical destruction of the body. For our discussion, we will continue to use three components (body, mind, and soul) to represent a human being, which aligns more directly with a physicalist's perspective.

Soul Survivor

The third and final component of a human being is the soul or spirit (including the concepts of a spiritual energy or vital force). It is the supersubtle body in Eastern civilizations. Interestingly, some religions teach that other living things such as animals, insects, and plants also have a soul or spirit/spiritual essence.

Wikipedia tells us that "the Modern English word soul is derived from Old English *sáwol* and is cognate with other German and Baltic terms for the same idea. The original concept is meant to be 'coming from or belonging to the sea/lake,' because of the German belief in souls being born out of and returning to sacred lakes."

5. *Wikipedia*, s.v. "Mind-Body Perspectives."

Most modern dictionaries define the soul as the spiritual or immaterial part of a human being. It is regarded as a distinct entity that exists separate from the body. The soul would be analogous to the software that runs your computer. When the software is installed, it is considered a part of the computer. However, the software exists separately from the computer. It can be uninstalled and transferred or downloaded onto another computer. Numerous religions declare that the soul—like computer software—can be downloaded onto or into another human body or other material object once its current body is destroyed. The soul is also generally considered to be immortal.

There are two schools of thought on the soul's immortality. Religious scholars draw a distinction between personal and collective immortality.

Personal immortality means that each human being's soul is personally and individually immortal.

Collective immortality argues that personal immortality does not exist. Only collective immortality is possible. It advances a position that all souls are part of the collective universe of spirits and ultimately the Supreme Being. But only the Supreme Being is immortal. Human beings' individual souls achieve immortality once they unite or reunite—and become one— with the Supreme Being. Most religions that support a philosophy of collective immortality also believe that all human souls will eventually unite or reunite with the Supreme Being.

Therefore, effectively the human soul is considered immortal, either on its own or in union with all other souls as part of the Supreme Being. While the soul is widely regarded as immortal, that is by no means a universal belief. The debate has been ongoing for thousands of years, and will no doubt continue for many years and may never be fully resolved.

Reverend John Haynes Holmes—the well-known pastor of the Community Church of New York from 1919 to 1949 and a founding member of the National Association for the Advancement of Colored People (NAACP) and the American Civil Liberties Union (ACLU)—put forth ten reasons to support the belief in the soul's immortality. He laid out his rationale in *The Affirmation of Immortality (The Ingersoll Lecture on the Immortality of Man for 1946)*. The speech was delivered at his alma mater, Harvard College, that same year.

Reverend Holmes's lecture could have been in response to Clarence Darrow's 1929 book *The Myth of Immortality*. Darrow argues that there is no evidence upon which to build a positive belief in immortality.

But, if the soul does live on after the destruction of the physical body, what happens to it?

Reflections

How well do you take care of your body (diet, exercise, grooming, etc.)?

When was the last time you stretched your mind to solve a complex problem or wrestle with a foreign concept?

How do you feed your soul?

4

Fundamental Truths

The truth is incontrovertible. Malice may attack it,
ignorance may deride it, but in the end, there it is.
—WINSTON CHURCHILL

An error does not become truth by reason of multiplied propagation,
nor does truth become error because nobody sees it.
—MAHATMA GANDHI

If you would be a real seeker after truth, it is necessary that at least once
in your life you doubt, as far as possible, all things.
—RENÉ DESCARTES

WE LEARNED IN THE last chapter that the soul is considered the immortal part of a human being. If the soul is incapable of being destroyed, what happens to it after the death of the physical body? So, when asking The Question—"What will happen to me when I die?"—we are really asking "What will happen to my soul (spirit, mind, consciousness, energy, force, etc.—whatever you call that part of a human being which survives death) when my physical body perishes?"

Well, before we can address The Question intelligently, we must first set a firm foundation.

Ground Zero

Any civil engineer will tell you that without a solid foundation, the structure—whether a house, bridge, or skyscraper—will eventually come tumbling down. Think of it this way. Truth is the foundation of knowledge. Knowledge is the building blocks of wisdom. And wisdom leads to understanding. Our foundation, upon which we must build to gain enough knowledge, wisdom, and understanding to answer The Question, is laid by accepting two fundamental truths. First, everyone is going to die, that is, cease to exist in their current physical form. Second, no one knows what will happen to them after they die.

I encourage you to take a break and think—I mean *really* think—about these two statements. Stop. Put down this book. Eliminate all distractions. Be quiet and be still for at least a few minutes.

༄ ༄

Ok. Let's resume.

The great Chinese philosopher Confucius once said, "If we don't know life, how can we know death?"

On the surface it appears that fundamental truth #1, Everyone is going to die, would be straightforward and unanimously accepted. However, not everyone believes this to be a true statement today or throughout history.

In the early development of Taoism,[1] practiced mainly in China, followers believed that a human being could attain physical immortality. The religion said little if anything about the afterlife because its adherents hoped never to die. Over the course of time, as the Chinese became exposed to peoples from different countries, cultures, and religions due to humans traveling and exploring their world, this concept of physical immortality slowly faded away. With no evidence—after thousands of years—of any follower ever attaining the goal, it became proof that the goal was unachievable.

However, for followers of Rastafarianism,[2] this concept of physical immortality is still a current belief within the religion. Rastafarians (also referred to as Rastas) do not believe in an afterlife. They do believe that a few select individuals will live forever here on earth in their current body or their spiritual body.

---

1. *Patheos*, "Taoism," §Beliefs: Afterlife and Salvation.

2. Answers.com, s.v. "What Do Rastafarians Believe?," https://www.answers.com/Q/What_do_rastafarians_believe_about_the_afterlife.

Of the twenty-two major religions (including some ideologies that may be classified as a nonreligion) identified in a 2012 analysis by Adherents.com,[3] Rastafarianism is the only religion that espoused such a belief. According to the United Nations and elaborated by *Worldometers*, world population in 2012 was 7.128 billion. With 600,000 individuals identified as Rastas, we can conclude that over 99.99 percent of the world's population accepts fundamental truth #1 as a fact.

On a pragmatic level, we can approach the assertion of fundamental truth #1 from our own personal experience. Ask yourself, "Who is the oldest person you know or have known personally?" For me, it would be Aunt Ethel on my mother's side. She was nicknamed Sister. Sister lived 101 years before leaving this earth on Independence Day in the summer of 2011. Who is it for you? If I were a betting man, I would be willing to make a wager that you do not personally know anyone who has lived more than 150 years.

Next, we could ask ourselves who have we heard of or read about in history that lived the longest. The historical figure I would point to is Methuselah from the book of Genesis in the Hebrew Bible (Judaism) and the Holy Bible (Christianity). Methuselah lived 969 years before departing this earth. Now granted that is a very, very long time for a human being to live. Nevertheless, he did indeed die.

So, from both angles, I hope you feel comfortable accepting it as a fact that every human being is going to die, that is, cease to exist in their current physical form. At this time, I am not addressing the possibility of rebirth or reincarnation, which will be discussed later in more detail.

Now let's turn to fundamental truth #2: No one knows what will happen to them after they die. This one is not as straightforward.

For starters, it goes against one of the six core needs that we have as human beings according to author, philanthropist, and self-help guru Anthony "Tony" Robbins. In his book *The Driving Force: The Six Human Needs*, the first need identified is *certainty*—the need for safety, stability, security, comfort, order, predictability, control, and consistency. For us to accept fundamental truth #2 as a fact, we will certainly have to set aside our desire to fulfill this need in an area where we desperately want concrete answers.

3. "Adherents.com: Religion Statistics Geography, Church Statistics" (Library of Congress web archive), p. 1, https://www.loc.gov/item/lcwaN0003960/.

Many people claim to know what happens to human beings after death, and therefore, they know what will happen to themselves specifically. Let's explore these claims more closely. We begin by examining the word *know*.

What does it mean to "know" something? *Webster's Dictionary* defines the word as such:

a. *Be aware of through observation, inquiry, or information—most people know that CFCs [chlorofluorocarbons] can damage the ozone layer*

b. *Have knowledge or information concerning—I would write to him if I knew his address*

c. *Be absolutely certain or sure about something—I just knew it was something I wanted to do*

d. *Have developed a relationship with (someone) through meeting and spending time with them; be familiar or friendly with—he knew and respected Laura*

e. *Have a good command of (a subject or language)*

f. *Recognize (someone or something)—Isabel couldn't hear the words clearly, but she knew the voice*

g. *Be familiar or acquainted with (something)—a little restaurant she knew near Times Square*

h. *Have personal experience of (an emotion or situation)—a man who had known better times*

i. *Regard or perceive as having a specified characteristic—he is also known as an amateur painter*

j. *Give (someone or something) a particular name or title—the doctor was universally known as "Hubert"*

k. *Be able to distinguish one person or thing from (another)—you are convinced you know your own baby from any other in the world*

l. *Have sexual intercourse with (someone)*

Comparing the word's various meanings, definition *h* is the most applicable in the context of the second fundamental truth. It could be argued that definition *c* also applies. However, to *"be absolutely certain or sure about"* what will happen to you after you die would point you back to definition *h* to gain that level of certainty or assurance.

Simply asked: Do you have personal experience of what will happen to you after you die? Or said another way, have you died and come back to life? Now here, we are not referring to a near-death experience (NDE) or someone who was in a coma, no matter what the length of time, then regained consciousness. We would like to know if you died for a significant amount of time—say at least three months—then came back to life. How is this different from someone having an NDE (for a few minutes, hours, or days) or lingering in a coma before regaining consciousness? Let's first consider an NDE.

Close Encounters

We can evaluate the case of an individual gaining knowledge through an NDE from two perspectives. First, let's assume someone else had the NDE and then we interview the person to gain knowledge and an understanding of their experience. The other perspective is for someone to personally have had an NDE. The second perspective provides us with the best chance of answering The Question and meets the criteria of definition h. In either case, we take at face value the individual is telling the truth about their experience. Therefore, we will approach the topic from the second perspective where the individual personally experienced an NDE.

In 1992, a Gallup poll estimated 13 million Americans, which equated to 5 percent of the US population at the time, had experienced an NDE.[4] Considered an international authority and recognized as one of the original researchers in the field of near-death studies, Dr. P. M. H. Atwater is one of the leading researchers in this area.

> P. M. H. Atwater has identified four distinctive types of NDEs. She discovered elements similar to those described by Moody and Ring but different patterning from what was billed as the classical version; each pattern type was accompanied by a subtle psychological profile suggestive of other forces that might be present. These four types have consistently held up throughout two decades of interviews, observations, and analysis regardless of a person's age, education, gender, culture, or religion. In her book, *Beyond the Light*, P. M. H. Atwater used separate chapters to discuss each of the four types. Below is a shorter rendition of the scenario patterns.

4. Dr. Jeff, "NDEs in United States?"

a. Initial Experience (Sometimes referred to as the "nonexperience")

Involves elements such as a loving nothingness, the living dark, a friendly voice, or a brief out-of-body episode. Usually experienced by those who seem to need the least amount of evidence for proof of survival, or who need the least amount of shakeup in their life at that point in time. Often, this becomes a "seed" experience or an introduction to other ways of perceiving and recognizing reality. Incident rate: 76% with child experiencers, 20% with adult experiencers.

b. Unpleasant or Hell-like Experience (Inner cleansing and self-confrontation)

Encounter with a threatening void or stark limbo or hellish purgatory, or scenes of a startling and unexpected indifference, even "hauntings" from one's own past. Usually experienced by those who seem to have deeply suppressed or repressed guilt, fears, and angers and/or those who expect some kind of punishment or discomfort after death. Incident rate: 3% with child experiencers, 15% with adult experiencers.

c. Pleasant or Heaven-like Experience (Reassurance and self-validation)

Heaven-like scenarios of loving family reunions with those who have died previously, reassuring religious figures or light beings, validation that life counts, affirmative and inspiring dialogue. Usually experienced by those who most need to know how loved they are and how important life is and how every effort has a purpose in the overall scheme of things. Incident rate: 19% with child experiencers, 47% with adult experiencers.

d. Transcendent Experience (Expansive revelations, alternate realities)

Exposure to otherworldly dimensions and scenes beyond the individual's frame of reference; sometimes includes revelations of greater truths. Seldom personal in content. Usually experienced by those who are ready for a mind-stretching challenge and/or individuals who are more apt to utilize (to whatever degree) the truths that are revealed to them. Incident rate: 2% with child experiencers, 18% with adult experiencers.[5]

---

5. Note: P. M. H. Atwater has noticed that all four types can occur at the same time during an NDE, can exist in varying combinations, or can spread out across a series of episodes for a particular individual. Generally speaking, however, each represents a

Let's suppose our NDE was a pleasant one. Surely now we could answer The Question having personally experienced death and come back to life. Right? I assert that we still would not be adequately equipped to know what will happen to us when we die. The expression, "Close, but no cigar," comes to mind.

Having an NDE is not the same as dying and staying dead for at least three months. At some point during our pleasurable NDE, we would see a bright light. This could happen instantly or after a few hours or even days. There may be various encounters or experiences along the way. These encounters or experiences could be with deceased loved ones, animals, friendly strangers, or time spent alone on a blissful journey. The light would be at the end of a tunnel, in the sky, or simply at some distance away from us. There may or may not be human-like figures in the light. We, or to be more precise, our soul, would be torn between going to the light and returning to our body back on earth. Inevitably our soul would return to our earthly body.

Had our soul continued to the light and stayed with the light, we would have in fact died and stayed dead. We would not have been able to relate our NDE to those still here on earth among the living. What awaits us in the light is still an unknown.

And even if our soul went to the light and experienced it, but then chose to return to our earthly body, we still would not know what will happen to us when we die. What we would know is what happened to us during this one specific instance while we were near death or even clinically dead. The knowledge would be limited to a discrete, individual NDE. Some individuals reported having multiple NDEs which were not all the same. They recalled a pleasurable NDE during one encounter and a distressing one on the next encounter or vice versa.

Whether NDEs can provide us with answers to The Question is best addressed by someone who has lived through an NDE.

Dr. George Rodonaia holds an M.D. and a Ph.D. in neuropathology, and a Ph.D. in the psychology of religion. He recently delivered a keynote address to the United Nations on the "Emerging Global Spirituality." Before immigrating to the United States from the Soviet Union in 1989, he worked as a research psychiatrist at the University of Moscow. Dr. Rodonaia underwent one of the most extended cases of a clinical near-death experience ever recorded. Pronounced

---

distinctive type of experience occurring but once to a given person.

29

dead immediately after he was hit by a car in 1976, he was left for three days in a morgue. He did not return to life until a doctor began to make an incision in his abdomen as part of an autopsy.[6]

Here are Dr. Rodonaia's closing remarks regarding his NDE.

Many people turn to those who have had near death experiences because they sense we have the answers. But I know this is not true, at least not entirely. None of us will fully fathom the great truths of life until we finally unite with eternity at death. But in the meantime, it is our very nature to seek answers to our deepest questions about the near-death experience and immortality.[78]

Let's Make a Deal

Allow me to make the point by way of a joke I once heard. A young man was given a unique opportunity to tour heaven and hell while still alive. He first chose to visit heaven, and it lived up to everything he had heard about the place. The streets were paved with gold. The landscape stretched endlessly with lush green rolling hills. The temperature was ideal. The music was pleasant, and the food was divine.

He then went to hell, and it was nothing like he expected. The streets were also paved with gold and diamonds. The landscape stretched endlessly with lush green rolling hills and beautiful clear waterfalls. The temperature was a pleasant, sunny seventy-seven degrees Fahrenheit. The music was peaceful. The food was delicious, and the people were relaxed and happy. Confused, the young man asked to speak with the person in charge.

"What am I seeing?" the young man asked Lucifer. "This is not what I was expecting." "Well," said Satan, "what were you expecting?" "I've been taught that hell is a place of torment. The temperature can reach 1,200 degrees Fahrenheit. There is no water. And the inhabitants are in constant pain and agony as punishment for their misdeeds while on earth." "Well, as you can see, that is not true," said Satan. "Don't listen to those people who have been feeding you tales about this place. They only want to keep you

6. Long and Long, "Dr. George Rodonaia."

7. Long and Long, "Dr. George Rodonaia."

8. You can read the full account of Dr. Rodonaia's near-death experience at https://www.nderf.org/Experiences/1george_rodonaia_nde.html, which is maintained by the Near-Death Experience Foundation.

from coming here and potentially taking their spot, since we only have a limited number of spots. Go back to earth and live your life in a way that guarantees your spot in hell is secure," advised Satan.

And that's exactly what the young man did. When he died, he could not wait to get to hell. Upon his arrival, he was once again confused.

He asked to talk with the person in charge. "What seems to be the problem?" Satan asked. "What am I seeing?" the young man asked. "The last time I was here the streets were paved with gold and diamonds. The landscape stretched endlessly with lush green rolling hills and beautiful clear waterfalls. The temperature was a pleasant, sunny seventy-seven degrees Fahrenheit. The music was peaceful. The food was delicious, and the people were relaxed and happy.

"Now the streets are black as charcoal with steam rising from them. The landscape is volcanic with molten lava running everywhere. There is no food or water. All the people are in constant agony. And it must be a thousand degrees Fahrenheit!" he shouted.

"Hmm, when were you here?" Satan asked calmly. He thought for a moment then the young man blurted out, "It was January 1st in the year 2000." "Aha that explains it. You were here for our gillennium celebration. We do that once every billion years. Every other day, it's like you see it now. Welcome to hell," said Satan.

Only You

All joking aside, we must admit that being near something is not the same as being there. On game day is being near the stadium the same as being in the stadium? If you have a condo three blocks from the boardwalk with an ocean view, is it the same as having a condo on the beach? As an athlete, is being on the sidelines the same as being in the middle of the action come game day? Is sitting in the passenger's seat of a high-performance sports car the same as being in the driver's seat, deliberately shifting gears with a firm grip on the steering wheel, feeling the split-second engagement and disengagement of the limited-slip differential as it provides optimal torque to the tires hugging the road, while you race along the winding, hairpin turns of Highway 101 up the pacific coast from Los Angeles to Santa Barbara—the sun clinging to its last vestige of brilliance above the mountain tops before the moon pushes its way into the evening sky? I think not.

Now someone could argue that they did in fact die, although it may have been for a moment. Therefore, they do know exactly what happened to them after death; and they would be correct. They do know what happened to them briefly after death. Emphasis on the word brief.

It would be like running the first few feet of a marathon and proclaiming to know what it's like to run the entire 26.2 miles. Imagine a newborn baby professing to know as much about life as someone a hundred years old after only sixty seconds in this world. As human beings, we require personal experience to acquire knowledge of certain subjects or situations. And the answer to The Question falls into that category. It's not something you can imagine, assume, forecast, or live vicariously through someone else, even if that someone else is your doppelgänger. You must personally do it.

What Dreams May Come

Now let's consider someone in a coma. According to *Wikipedia*, "In medicine a coma (from the Greek κῶμα *koma*, meaning deep sleep) is a state of unconsciousness, lasting more than 6 hours in which a person cannot be awakened, fails to respond normally to painful stimuli, light or sound, lacks a normal sleep-wake cycle and does not initiate voluntary actions. A person in a state of coma is described as comatose. According to the Glasgow Coma Scale though, a person with confusion is considered to be in the mildest coma."[9]

From its definition, a coma is more akin to sleep than to death. Therefore, a coma would be further from dying than an NDE, where an individual can be clinically dead. We have already concluded that an NDE does not meet our expanded requirements to be dead (i.e., three months or longer). So, we can conclude that a person lingering in a coma would not satisfy these requirements. Whatever a person experienced during a coma would be most accurately categorized as a dream. Or even perhaps an out-of-body experience (OBE). But not death. This of course, does not rule out the possibility that someone in a coma may die—once or multiple times—during their comatose state. And then rejoin the land of the living. During these momentary deaths, if the individual had any experiences, they would be classified as NDEs.

9. *Wikipedia*, s.v. "Coma."

Fundamental Truths

A reasonable question one might ask is whether an OBE can shed any light on The Question. Perhaps it can shed some light but will not allow a definitive answer. And in my personal case, it did not.

It was March 2, 1997, the eve of my thirty-third birthday. I was single at the time and didn't have any grand plans for the following day. Growing up in a family the size of two baseball teams, we had never made a big deal about birthdays. I suppose part of the reason was because there were seventeen children and my family did not have much money. Regardless of the reason, I had come to view my birthday as just another day. Well, as I crawled into bed that night, little did I know that this birthday would not be just like any other one.

As I dozed off to sleep, I started to dream. At least I assumed I was dreaming because the next things I experienced surely could not happen in real life.

I found myself in the company of two children. They appeared to be around seven or eight years of age. One was a girl and the other was a boy. Each was holding one of my hands. Not that it mattered, but it struck me as odd that I could not discern the children's ethnicity. They were not talking, but I felt a sense of joy from them that made it clear they were happy to be with me. They were with me in my bedroom at that moment, but then instantaneously we were in another place. I don't know how we got there.

It was a large room with hardwood floors, and the three of us were playing together. Well, to be more accurate, the children were playing, and I was watching them. The room had an enormous bay window. It reminded me of an apartment in Worcester, Massachusetts, I had rented after graduating from college in the summer of 1986. Worcester is home of the Eastern Association of Rowing Colleges' (EARC) annual Eastern Sprints held at Regatta Point on Lake Quinsigamond in mid- to late May. I had competed there for four years as a coxswain on the Yale Men's Lightweight Crew Team. Wonderful memories.

I could hear the clanking sound of the children's shoes. It echoed throughout the apartment. There was no furniture. What I assumed was light from the sun illuminated the room through the big bay window. The light danced gracefully across the polished wooden floors. And the air was filled with the most enticing aroma of cinnamon, apples, and ginger.

While the children laughed and played, the three of us were engaged in a conversation. However, we were not using our mouths to talk. It was as if we were reading each other's thoughts and responding. The topic of discussion was what happens to humans when they die. I had lots of questions. They didn't answer my questions, but continually assured me that I would get answers. In fact, they looked forward to being able to provide me with the knowledge I sought.

Then I heard a man's voice, which seemed to originate from another room—what would have been the kitchen if it had been my apartment after college—say, "You have to take him back. It's not time." The children responded, "But he had questions." "I know, but you must take him back," the voice insisted. The man's voice was gentle yet firm like a caring father. Reluctantly, the children took my hands once again and instantly we were back in my bedroom, looking down at my body on the bed. I lingered there for a moment and gazed around the room. It looked different from that vantage point. I don't recall reuniting with my body, and then suddenly I was awake.

I sat up in bed and tried to understand what had just happened. Was I dreaming or had something else occurred? It didn't feel like a dream. To this day, I can't say with absolute certainty if what I experienced was a dream or an OBE. After all I was alone, so I couldn't ask anyone if they saw or heard anything that would point me in one direction or the other. But if you ask me, I will tell you that it was an OBE. And I also believe I know what led to the event.

As I stated before, I have been asking myself The Question for many years. During that specific time of my life, I found myself searching very earnestly, and probably more intensely than any time before for answers. My mother was very ill—after years of battling diabetes, high blood pressure, and other ailments, some a by-product of the physical, mental, and emotional abuse inflicted by her husband, not to mention the stress sixteen separate childbirths over a twenty-year period had placed on her body— and I didn't think she would live much longer. As it turned out, I was right. Dee La left this world a few months later.

Now as I said earlier, the children never answered my questions regarding the afterlife. But what if they had? Would I then be able to say that I now know what will happen to me when I die? Sadly, the answer is still no. I could say that I was told or shown what will happen to me when I die, and I believe it. I would not know it to be a fact until I died and personally experienced it in death.

Anyone who has had an OBE and came back to their body to tell about it, can relay their experience to others. But that experience no matter how profound or compelling is not adequate to answer The Question. An

OBE is a first cousin to an NDE. During an OBE, the person has not died. Therefore, if an NDE—where a person is clinically dead—cannot answer The Question, then an OBE would not be able to either.

Interview with a Spirit

The other definition of the word *know* that may be stretched to have some applicability in the context of fundamental truth #2 is *a*:

a. *Be aware of through observation, inquiry, or information—most people know that CFCs [chlorofluorocarbons] can damage the ozone layer*

We would ask, have you personally observed someone die and come back to life, or has a dead person been in communication with you? If the answer is yes, then we would need objective evidence. Through a series of questions and other information you gathered from the individual, you would be able to answer The Question. Right?

For you to answer yes to the first question—Have you personally observed someone die and come back to life?—we would need verifiable evidence that the person identified had died for at least three months, and then came back to life. Such a case does not currently exist nor has there ever been one documented. Therefore, it's safe to conclude that no one would be able to offer the necessary proof to support an answer in the affirmative to this question.

For you to answer yes to the second question—Has a dead person been in communication with you?—it would need to be proven that the dead person is communicating with you, the person still alive, which is a near impossibility.

Interestingly, this very ability is one of the fundamental tenets of Spiritism (also referred to as Spiritualism) by means of a medium. The religion's modern-day origins began in 1848 with Maggie and Katie Fox. The sisters started communicating with spirits through rappings in their house in Hydesville, New York. Since then, individuals have reportedly presented scientific evidence that such communications exist. However, not everyone has been convinced.

One of the most famous individuals to doubt the authenticity of communication with the dead was Ehrich Weiss, born Erik Weisz, and better known as Harry Houdini (1874–1926).

Houdini contended that thought is a function of the brain, and death consists of the cessation of life activities, with nothing beyond. He also maintained that his training and experience had led him to the conclusion that communications with spirits were purely human fabrications, all delusion and trickery.

Before his death Houdini made a pact with his wife, as a last test of Spiritualism; if spirit survival was possible, he would communicate with her by a series of coded messages. She attended various séances in order to receive messages from him, but after years of trying to communicate through Spiritualism with her husband without any result, she declared the experiment a failure.[10]

Although the Fox sisters confessed that their ability was a hoax,[11] for argument's sake, let's assume Houdini was wrong. That in fact communication with the dead is possible. What the dead person would be experiencing is specific to him. There is no way of knowing, based on our understanding of the word *know*, or proving that you will have the same experience as the dead person when you die. So, this still would not allow The Question to be answered. As with my personal OBE, had the children answered my questions, you could say that you were told what will happen to you when you die, and you believe it. You would not know it to be a fact until you died and personally experienced it in death.

Knowing

Now with that settled, let's talk about the difference between what someone knows and what they believe. At first glance, it may seem to be a topic that does not warrant much discussion. The difference is obvious. Isn't it?

There is a pervasive tendency throughout the world, and especially the Western Hemisphere, to use these words synonymously. And that is an extremely dangerous practice. I believe you know what I mean.

You should be able to prove something that is known; so that it's established as a fact. In a civil court of law, the plaintiff is required to present a preponderance of evidence to prove her case. The evidence can be any combination of eyewitness testimony and/or overwhelming empirical data. In a criminal proceeding, the prosecutor must prove his case beyond

---

10. Lewis, *Encyclopedia of Afterlife Beliefs*, 191.
11. Abbott, "Fox Sisters on Spiritualism."

a reasonable doubt. And in the scientific arena, experiments are often conducted to collect factual data to prove or disprove a theory.

A belief, while it may be held in one's own perception as the truth, may not in fact be true. Also, because a belief is widely shared among many individuals, does not make it true. There are many examples that can be presented to support this argument but let me point to one that is probably familiar to most of us.

> The concept of a spherical Earth displaced earlier beliefs in a flat Earth: In early Mesopotamian mythology, the world was portrayed as a flat disk floating in the ocean with a hemispherical sky-dome above, and this forms the premise for early world maps like those of Anaximander and Hecataeus of Miletus. Other speculations on the shape of Earth include a seven-layered ziggurat or cosmic mountain, alluded to in the Avesta and ancient Persian writings (see seven climes).
>
> The earliest documented mention of the spherical Earth concept dates from around the 5th century BC, when it was mentioned by ancient Greek philosophers. In the 3rd century BC, Hellenistic astronomy established the roughly spherical shape of the Earth as a physical fact and calculated the Earth's circumference. This knowledge was gradually adopted throughout the Old World during Late Antiquity and the Middle Ages. A practical demonstration of Earth's sphericity was achieved by Ferdinand Magellan and Juan Sebastián Elcano's circumnavigation (1519–1522).[12]

Here's another example from my personal experience. Not long ago I met one of my wife's older brothers. Everyone (eyewitness testimony) calls him Terry. I asked her why people called him by that name, since his given name was Thomas. She replied that Terry was his middle name, and he was named after their father. Her father and brother's full names were Thomas Terry Winston and Thomas Terry Winston II. To distinguish them from one another, some people called her father Thomas and her brother Terry. However, within the family, they were both called Terry. Then she chuckled and said there was an interesting story behind it. "Do tell," I insisted.

Well, everyone referred to her father as Thomas Terry. In fact, her father referred to himself this way, as well. He thought that was his given name. He was obviously convinced—and "certain"—of his name since he gave his son the same name. It wasn't until late in his life that he discovered the truth.

---

12. *Wikipedia*, s.v. "Spherical Earth."

Gambling With Your Soul

At around sixty years of age, her father went to increase his life insurance coverage and was required to present his birth certificate. After obtaining his first officially certified birth certificate, he learned that his given name was Thomas Elmer Winston. Imagine his surprise.

So, what my father-in-law and the people who knew him had formulated in their minds was a belief that his name was Thomas Terry Winston. However, that was not a fact, and consequently not the truth. Only upon examining his birth certificate (empirical data) could they get to a preponderance of evidence, which was also beyond a reasonable doubt—since it was an officially certified document, and then arrive at the truth—the non-negotiable foundation required to build knowledge.

Consider the following case.

> Ronald Cotton's story begins on a summer night in 1984, when two rapes were committed in Burlington, North Carolina. In each case, an assailant entered an apartment, cut the phone wires, raped a woman at knifepoint, and stole money and other items. Both victims were taken to the hospital, where full rape examination kits were completed.
>
> The first victim, 22-year-old Jennifer Thompson, described her attacker as a tall African-American man in his early 20s. Police collected photographs of area men meeting that description, including 22-year-old Ronald Cotton, a Burlington resident employed at a restaurant near Thompson's apartment. Cotton had two prior convictions: one for breaking and entering, and another for assault with intent to rape. Thompson selected Cotton from police photos as her rapist. When Cotton visited the police station to clear up the misunderstanding, he only strengthened the case mounting against him. He claimed that he had been with friends on the night of the rapes, but those friends did not corroborate his alibi. At a physical lineup of suspects, Thompson again selected Cotton. In August 1984, police arrested Cotton and took him into custody. In January 1985, Cotton was convicted of Thompson's rape and sentenced to life in prison. That verdict, however, was overturned, and a new trial was ordered. Cotton was optimistic given a crucial discovery he had made about one of his fellow inmates, Bobby Poole—a tall African-American young man from Burlington also convicted of rape who bore a strong resemblance to the composite sketch used in Cotton's case. Poole had reportedly bragged to inmates that he had committed the rapes for which Cotton was serving time.

The second trial was even more devastating than the first. Both victims testified against Cotton; the jury did not believe that Poole was the real assailant; and, most damaging of all, the court withheld evidence of Poole's alleged confessions. Convicted of both rapes, Cotton received two life sentences plus 55 years in prison.

Back in prison, Cotton "waited it out" for years. In 1994, however, he learned about DNA testing (a procedure unavailable at the time of his trials). He filed and won a motion for DNA testing. In 1995, Burlington police turned over to the court all case evidence containing semen or other bodily fluids. Samples from Jennifer Thompson had deteriorated and could not be tested, but those from the second victim provided a breakthrough for Cotton. On a tiny vaginal swab, scientists found a bit of sperm. Subjected to PCR [Polymerase Chain Reaction] testing, that sample showed no match to Ronald Cotton. He could not have committed the crime.

The state DNA database matched the sample to Bobby Poole. On June 30, 1995, almost 11 years after the rapes and 10 1/2 years after being taken into custody, Ronald Cotton was cleared of all charges and released from prison.[13]

Over the past half century, each successive generation—Generation X (Gen-X), Generation Y (also known as the Millennial Generation), and Generation Z (sometimes referred to as Generation ADD)—has more strongly embraced the idea that an individual can create their own reality. The media began experimenting with what's become known as Reality TV in the late 1940s. But it wasn't until the 1990s and early 2000s that the format exploded into a global phenomenon with the success of *Survivor*, *Idols*, and *Big Brother*.[14]

The participants are not actors or actresses. The premise of the show is to allow the viewer to see a person's behavior without following a script from a writer. It's meant to offer a realistic take on life by the individual, group, family, or team being watched.

The shows have great appeal and have grown in popularity. I suspect—at least in part—their success is due to our fascination with human behavior. It's interesting to see what people do or say in a situation based on their natural instincts without "acting." This is believed to give the viewer a truer picture of reality, and I agree. But as "real" as the show appears, the camera is rolling. And many years of scientific research has demonstrated that living

13. US Department of Justice, "Proof of Innocence."
14. *Wikipedia*, s.v. "Reality Television."

creatures—especially human beings, as well as many animals—behave differently when they know that someone or something is watching them.

A Real Illusion

The bigger problem arises when we assume everything that's real is also true. A lie can be very real. But it's still a lie. And that's the truth. We must guard against blurring the line between reality and truth and acting as if they are the same. They are not. Albert Einstein once noted, "Reality is merely an illusion, albeit a very persistent one."

It's been said that perception is reality. Well, it is for that specific individual. However, that person's reality does not mean it is the truth. Consider the scenario of a person who is color-blind.

Dichromats are individuals who often confuse red and green items. For example, they may find it difficult to distinguish a Braeburn (red) apple from a Granny Smith (green) or the red and green colors of a traffic light. Suppose you are in a traffic accident with a dichromat, who is unaware of his condition. After ensuring no one is injured, you and the driver of the other vehicle begin to discuss the unfortunate situation.

"Why did you go through the light?" you ask him. He responds that his light was green, and he had the right of way. "That's not correct," you insist. "My light was green, and your light was red." The dichromat responds, "No. I am certain. My light was green, and your light was red." Realizing that the two of you are not going to see eye to eye, you involve the other passengers.

You were alone, while he has four other passengers in his vehicle. One by one, they all agree that the light for them was green and the light for you was red. Well, you think to yourself, "Of course the passengers in his car are going to agree with him." But they all seem like genuinely honest people, and it's clear they firmly believe what they are saying is true. What you don't know is that all five individuals in the other vehicle are dichromats, who are unaware of their condition.

Convinced you are correct, you notice a dozen or so pedestrians who witnessed the accident, so you get them involved. "Excuse me, miss, we seem to have a disagreement regarding the incident. I was hoping you could tell us what you observed that led to the accident."

The young lady is reluctant to get involved, but she did see the whole thing. "I am sorry to tell you, sir, but I saw you go through a red light." And one by one, all the pedestrians report they saw the same thing. "What the

____? This is crazy," you think to yourself. Now you start to wonder if you got it wrong.

Was the light for you red and green for the other driver? Were you momentarily distracted or did your mind wonder off? You had not been drinking. You were not tired, talking on the phone, or texting. It was a clear summer evening, without a cloud in the sky, and you were—as it so happened—going the speed limit. There was nothing that would explain why you mistook a red light to be green.

It never even crossed your mind that everyone, besides yourself, at the scene of the accident was color-blind. Furthermore, the dichromats were unaware of their own condition; so, they had no reason to suspect that their perception of the colors red and green may not be accurate. Just as serious doubt is starting to creep into your mind, two police officers arrive at the scene. Thank goodness, you think, now we can get to the truth.

The officers proceed to question everyone, but to your disappointment, the stories all stay the same. After getting everyone's eyewitness testimony, the officers come to you. "Sir, it appears that you made a mistake and ran through a red light causing the accident. Everyone questioned reports that the light was red for you and green for the other driver. We believe this is truly what happened but give us a minute for one final confirmation."

The officers go back to their squad car. It is now standard protocol to review the camera images from video surveillance equipment installed at most intersections in major metropolitan cities. At this point, you are convinced that you somehow made a mistake. You don't know or understand how you could have, but it's becoming clear that you did.

The police officers return after a few minutes and call both you (Driver A) and the other driver (Driver B) together. "Gentlemen, we have a bit of a situation. The video evidence does not support the details provided by the eyewitnesses. It is clear the light was green for Driver A (you) and red for Driver B (the other driver)."

It Is What It Is . . . and That's All That It Is

As demonstrated by these examples, there is a profound difference between what one believes and what one knows. Several conclusions can be drawn:

1. The number of people who share a belief has no bearing on its truthfulness.

2. A belief can change over time as more knowledge is gained.

3. The truth remains the same forever.
   a.   It cannot be bribed or bargained with.
   b.   It has no interest in being politically correct.
   c.   It shows no respect to rank, position, or title.
   d.   It is not swayed by persuasive arguments.

4. The truth is an absolute fact.
   a.   It is color-blind.
   b.   It cares not for fame, fortune, or status.
   c.   It is not shaped by one's perception.

5. To know something is to know the truth—an absolute fact.

Through our analysis, we conclude that a person cannot know what will happen to them after death until they die . . .and stays dead.

Reflections

How has one of your beliefs changed over time as you gained more knowledge?

When were you surprised after learning the truth about something?

When was the last time you "knew" something was going to happen, but it didn't?

5

The Hereafters

Life is a journey. Death is a return to earth. The universe is like an inn.
The passing years are like dust. Regard this phantom world as a star at dawn,
a bubble in a stream, a flash of lightning in a summer cloud,
a flickering lamp—a phantom—and a dream.

—THE BUDDHA

Sell this life for the next and you win both of them.
Sell the next life for this one and you lose both of them.

—HASAN AL-BASRI

I regard the brain as a computer which will stop working when its
components fail. There is no heaven or afterlife for broken down computers;
that is a fairy story for people afraid of the dark.

—STEPHEN HAWKING

ACKNOWLEDGING THE DIFFERENCE BETWEEN knowing and believing, we
must answer the question: "What do people believe will happen to them after
they die?" This question is best addressed in the context of religious theologies. It's also important that we incorporate nonreligious points of view.

Throughout the course of history, there have been hundreds—if not
thousands—of different religious beliefs about the afterlife. Many are no

longer accepted by the current world population. But even today there remain numerous different views. In the previous chapter, we concluded that it's not possible to know what will happen to us prior to our actual death. As a result, each religious and nonreligious viewpoint has an equal probability of being correct. Now, to accept this as a valid concept and address the topic objectively, we must set aside—for the moment—our personal beliefs or experiences.

Cemented in the guiding philosophies of all religions—and many nonreligions—are two common foundational elements: a desire to do good, and a continuous quest for knowledge, wisdom, and understanding.

First, every religion encourages its followers to do good works and avoid bad or evil deeds. Accepting that an action starts first in the mind as a thought or even subconsciously as a motive, adherents are taught to have good thoughts and underlying intentions. These seeds will blossom into good words and good deeds. Appendix C provides a sample of behaviors considered especially evil or sinful by some of the world's most renowned religions. Followers are warned to avoid these acts. Of note, there is considerable alignment across religions on many evil or sinful acts. Some examples are adultery, dishonesty, envy, murder, pride, rape, slander, sloth, and theft.

Now certainly a person's good deeds do not need to stem from a religion's prompting. There are many reasons why an individual would do something good. You may be nice to someone because you are instinctively a nice person and that is the most natural way for you to act. On the other hand, being nice could be completely out of character for you. But today, you woke up on the opposite side of the bed and being nice to someone else just felt right—today. Or you might deliberately go out of your way to be nice to someone because you expect something in return—independent of your natural inclinations either toward or away from good deeds. In any given situation, your nice behavior may have nothing to do with your religious or nonreligious beliefs.

Second, every religion encourages its followers to pursue a path of knowledge and wisdom. The path leads to a higher level of understanding oneself, the world in which we live, and the greater universe. The terms used to describe this endeavor vary. Some religions refer to it as seeking enlightenment, while others call it becoming self-aware, spiritually aware, or undergoing a self-transformation. Various religions encourage us to be transformed by the renewing of our minds. And while there may be many paths to achieve this amount of knowledge and wisdom, the goal is basically the same. It is to gain a level of understanding—which will lead to acceptance—that all humans are connected. We have a bond with each other, and to some degree with every other living thing on earth and possibly within the entire universe.

Before delving into the different afterlife possibilities taught by the world's most followed religions—including some ideologies that may be classified as a nonreligion—(see appendix A: according to a 2012 estimate by Adherents.com), we must first address a key point that could otherwise make our discussion irrelevant.

We learned in chapter 3 that most scholars of today and throughout history regard the human soul as being immortal. If, however, the human soul is not immortal, then the question of what happens to it is meaningless. Whether the soul existed on planet earth or some other celestial body would be irrelevant. It would not make a difference if it lived out its existence in another realm, dimension, or spirit world. The soul could have occupied many different bodies—human, animal, insect, or some other species. At some point, regardless of the number of years, rebirths, or reincarnations, it would simply vanish. Now our goal is to determine the soul's final fate. What may happen to the soul between today and its ultimate destination is interesting but not our aim. As a result, if we knew for a fact the soul was not immortal, this book would end immediately. Full stop. Drop the mic.

However, since we must consider all possibilities to determine "The End" for a human being, both a mortal and immortal soul are included in our discussion and analysis. In the case where the human soul is immortal, the soul's objective is to obtain a good afterlife rather than a bad one. For our specific discussion, good is defined as a condition the soul desires, providing a feeling or sense of pleasure, peace, comfort, and the like. Bad is defined as a condition the soul does not desire, providing a feeling or sense of pain, suffering, discomfort, and the like.

Another aspect of The Question we will not address is the fate of an infant's soul. The child may have died in the womb, within a few days of birth, or after a few years. But in all cases before she was able to make a thoughtful, informed decision regarding her beliefs about religious matters. As might be expected, there's a spectrum of outcomes put forth. In the case of rebirth or reincarnation, the child's soul simply continues in the cycle of life, death, and rebirth. Theologies which believe in a final judgment have hope that an infant's soul would not experience any form of punishment or torment. This discussion is beyond the scope of this book.

Clueless

Not all religions have an official position regarding an afterlife. They simply do not address the question, profess openly that they do not know what happens to a person after death, or conclude that the question is not relevant. The religions that fall into this category—either entirely or a subset of its followers—include Secular/Nonreligious/Agnostic/Atheist, Chinese Traditional (Confucianism), Juche, and Unitarian Universalism (see appendix B). The group has approximately 145 million adherents representing 1.79 percent of the world's population.

Without a Trace

The first afterlife possibility we explore is one where there is no form of life after death. Once we expire from the physical world it's over. We disappear without a trace. Followers within the Secular/Nonreligious/Agnostic/Atheist, Chinese Traditional (Chinese Folk-Religionist), African Traditional & Diasporic, and Unitarian Universalism religions (see appendix B) hold this belief. Some specific groups within the religions do, however, admit to the possibility of an afterlife.

For instance, "A humanist [included within Secular/Nonreligious/Agnostic/Atheist] might accept the possibility of some sort of afterlife because, to be fair, we humans don't know everything yet. At the same time, it would be necessary to acknowledge that there is no evidence for it, that there is strong evidence against it, that its existence is therefore rather unlikely, and at any rate it just isn't relevant to the much more important issues that face us today in the world we know exists. That, in a nutshell, is the humanist perspective on an afterlife."[1]

There are approximately 1.024 billion adherents inside these religions—with this specific perspective—representing 12.63 percent of the world's population.

In this afterlife scenario there is nothing after death. No heaven or hell. No new world. No in-between world. No reincarnation or rebirth onto this planet or any other astronomical body. No new universe. No union or reunion with God, the Supreme Being, the eternal spirit, or spiritual beings of any sort. No part of us continues to exist, which means that whether we have a soul is irrelevant, because it also ceases to exist once we die. We

1. Cline, "What Is Secular Humanism?"

47

have no memory of our life on earth because we no longer have a memory, consciousness, or anything else. We simply vanish. Like a candle blown out, we disappear in every way.

If this were the reality of what awaits us after death, then clearly it does not matter how we live our lives while on earth. Neither our actions/ deeds—including intentions (whether good or bad/evil)—nor our beliefs (whether religious or nonreligious) during our lifetime, will have any bearing on our afterlife. In fact, the term afterlife is meaningless in this scenario.

There is no reward for being a good person and no punishment for being a bad person. How much or how little we accomplish on earth would also have no consequence to us. There would be no value to an individual becoming enlightened, self-aware, spiritually aware, or transformed by the renewing of their mind—in the pursuit of knowledge, wisdom, and understanding. The person would presumably be aware that nothing existed after death, and then upon his death succumb to the same fate as everyone else who was not enlightened. There would be no need for or value in receiving God's grace, which would also not be possible since God would not exist. In this afterlife reality, there is no distinction between a good afterlife and a bad afterlife because there is no such thing. Every human being is assured the same fate—nothingness.

Déjà Vu

The next afterlife possibility has no heaven and no hell. God(s) may or may not exist. The environment would be very much as it is today on earth except in a purely spiritual world(s) instead of a physical one. Traditional Shinto calls the most sacred of these "the other world of heaven."

Followers within several religions, including Secular/Nonreligious/ Agnostic/Atheist, Chinese Traditional (Chinese Folk-Religionist), Primal-Indigenous, African Traditional & Diasporic, Spiritism, Neopaganism, and Unitarian Universalism (see appendix B), hold this view. It is estimated that 592 million individuals have this belief, equating to 7.30 percent of the world's population.

What the soul accomplishes in this spiritual world will determine if it has a good or bad afterlife. It's perception of good and bad will also play a major role. The soul's starting position would not be the dominant factor in determining if it ultimately has a good or bad afterlife. From our physical world, we know that an individual can start out in a bad condition and move into a good condition. The reverse is also true. This could happen suddenly by way of luck—good or bad—or through a lifetime of focused effort. Furthermore, whatever a person's current condition, it need not be permanent. It can change—from good to bad or bad to good—many times throughout a person's life. With eternity as the soul's life span, it is not only possible but likely that a soul's condition will change many times during its existence.

Our actions/deeds—including intentions (whether good or bad/ evil)—and our beliefs (whether religious or nonreligious) during our life will have no lasting effect on our afterlife. These things may factor into our starting point in the spirit world but will not determine our ending condition.

There is no predetermined reward for a "good" person and no punishment destined for a "bad" person. How much or how little we accomplish in the physical world would be of no significance to us. There would be no benefit afforded to an individual who became enlightened. The person would presumably be aware that their soul will spend eternity in a spiritual world with no good or bad destination. And then upon her death proceed to that destination like everyone else who was not enlightened. There would be no need for or value in receiving God's grace if there was such a being. In this afterlife reality, attaining and maintaining a good afterlife would be subjective. All souls would have an equal opportunity and the same probability of achieving it—independent of their religious or nonreligious beliefs while they were alive.

The Merry-Go-Round

The next afterlife possibility is centered around the concept of reincarnation, rebirth, or transmigration. All three terms, with some slight variations across cultures, involve the soul returning to the physical or natural world. For simplicity, I will use the term rebirth to represent all three terms going forward.

Now the soul is not actually reborn. As stated earlier, it is widely held that the soul is immortal. Therefore, it is not the soul that experiences death and rebirth. The soul simply moves from one host body to another. It's the host body that dies. When a new host body is born, the soul merges—or is downloaded like computer software—with it for its next life or incarnation. It is the same soul.

For our purposes, the physical or natural world refers to the entire universe. It encompasses all planets, moons, stars, objects, and matter of any kind. These ideologies incorporate the possibility that an individual could be reborn onto another planet or some other celestial body. Also included is allowance for the soul to be reborn into something other than a human body. It provides three potential outcomes.

Ain't No Stopping Us Now

In the first outcome, there is no escape from the cycle of birth, death, and rebirth. It continues forever. No soul ever gets off the merry-go-round. The soul continues to be reborn (or more accurately, attached to a new host body) into the physical or natural world for all of eternity. In the religious theologies that hold this belief, there is no world other than the physical or natural living world. This living world does include other planets and astronomical bodies besides earth and spans the entire universe. Based on your unique and individual perspective, being reborn forever can be considered good or bad.

In the Western Hemisphere, where there is much focus on preserving one's life for as long as possible, rebirth is generally seen as being good. Indeed, some individuals and organizations have gone to great lengths to explore ways of preserving and one day bringing a person back to this physical world after their death—if not preventing death altogether. Ideas differ on how this might be achieved. There are four prevailing approaches.

1. The physical body is restored with the person's soul/mind/consciousness intact. This is the hope of those using cryonics to preserve their bodies.

2. The person's soul/mind/consciousness is captured—referred to as mind uploading or whole brain emulation (WBE)—and transferred into a cyborg—a being with both organic and biomechatronic body parts. This is the approach of the nonprofit organization the 2045 Initiative, founded by Russian entrepreneur Dmitry Itskov. "The main goal of the 2045 Initiative, as stated on its website, is 'to create technologies enabling the transfer of an individual's personality to a more advanced non-biological carrier, and extending life, including to the point of immortality. We devote particular attention to enabling the

fullest possible dialogue between the world's major spiritual traditions, science and society."[2]

3. The person's soul/mind/consciousness is captured and downloaded
into a computer where it achieves a kind of digital immortality. "Living" forever in a virtual reality. This path aligns with the idea of a
technological singularity, where the intelligence of supercomputers
surpasses all human intelligence.

4. Through advances in science and technology—specifically bio-
medical, a person would never die. Transhumanists advocate for the
transformation of a human being—into what's called a posthuman
being—with enhanced abilities that extend a person's life indefinitely.

Not all individuals or organizations doing research in this general area
are intent on achieving the above goals. However, their discoveries could
support, or even advance others' research that is focused on reviving a human being—or even preventing death in the first place.

The article's headline in the April 18, 2019, edition of the *Yale News*
reads, "Scientists Restore Some Functions in a Pig's Brain Hours after
Death."

> Circulation and cellular activity were restored in a pig's brain four
> hours after its death, a finding that challenges long-held assump-
> tions about the timing and irreversible nature of the cessation of
> some brain functions after death, Yale scientists report April 17 in
> the journal *Nature*.
>
> The brain of a postmortem pig obtained from a meatpack-
> ing plant was isolated and circulated with a specially designed
> chemical solution. Many basic cellular functions, once thought to
> cease seconds or minutes after oxygen and blood flow cease, were
> observed, the scientists report.
>
> "The intact brain of a large mammal retains a previously un-
> derappreciated capacity for restoration of circulation and certain
> molecular and cellular activities multiple hours after circulatory
> arrest," said senior author Nenad Sestan [named as one of *Nature's*
> ten scientists who made a difference in 2019], professor of neuro-
> science, comparative medicine, genetics, and psychiatry.
>
> However, researchers also stressed that the treated brain
> lacked any recognizable global electrical signals associated with
> normal brain function.

2. *Wikipedia*, s.v. "2045 Initiative."

Gambling With Your Soul

"At no point did we observe the kind of organized electrical activity associated with perception, awareness, or consciousness," said co-first author Zvonimir Vrselia, associate research scientist in neuroscience. "Clinically defined, this is not a living brain, but it is a cellularly active brain."

Cellular death within the brain is usually considered to be a swift and irreversible process. Cut off from oxygen and a blood supply, the brain's electrical activity and signs of awareness disappear within seconds, while energy stores are depleted within minutes. Current understanding maintains that a cascade of injury and death molecules are then activated leading to widespread, irreversible degeneration.

However, researchers in Sestan's lab, whose research focuses on brain development and evolution, observed that the small tissue samples they worked with routinely showed signs of cellular viability, even when the tissue was harvested multiple hours postmortem. Intrigued, they obtained the brains of pigs processed for food production to study how widespread this postmortem viability might be in the intact brain. Four hours after the pig's death, they connected the vasculature of the brain to circulate a uniquely formulated solution they developed to preserve brain tissue, utilizing a system they call BrainEx. They found neural cell integrity was preserved, and certain neuronal, glial, and vascular cell functionality was restored.

The new system can help solve a vexing problem—the inability to apply certain techniques to study the structure and function of the intact large mammalian brain—which hinders rigorous investigations into topics like the roots of brain disorders, as well as neuronal connectivity in both healthy and abnormal conditions.

"Previously, we have only been able to study cells in the large mammalian brain under static or largely two-dimensional conditions utilizing small tissue samples outside of their native environment," said co-first author Stefano G. Daniele, an M.D./Ph.D. candidate. "For the first time, we are able to investigate the large brain in three dimensions, which increases our ability to study complex cellular interactions and connectivity."

While the advance has no immediate clinical application, the new research platform may one day be able to help doctors find ways to help salvage brain function in stroke patients, or test the efficacy of novel therapies targeting cellular recovery after injury, the authors say.

The research was primarily funded by the National Institutes of Health's (NIH) BRAIN Initiative.

"This line of research holds hope for advancing understanding and treatment of brain disorders and could lead to a whole new way of studying the postmortem human brain," said Andrea Beckel-Mitchener, chief of functional neurogenomics at the NIH's National Institute of Mental Health, which co-funded the research.

The researchers said that it is unclear whether this approach can be applied to a recently deceased human brain. The chemical solution used lacks many of the components natively found in human blood, such as the immune system and other blood cells, which makes the experimental system significantly different from normal living conditions. However, the researcher stressed any future study involving human tissue or possible revival of global electrical activity in postmortem animal tissue should be done under strict ethical oversight.

"Restoration of consciousness was never a goal of this research," said co-author Stephen Latham, director of Yale's Interdisciplinary Center for Bioethics. "The researchers were prepared to intervene with the use of anesthetics and temperature-reduction to stop organized global electrical activity if it were to emerge. Everyone agreed in advance that experiments involving revived global activity couldn't go forward without clear ethical standards and institutional oversight mechanisms."

"There is an ethical imperative to use tools developed by the Brain Initiative to unravel mysteries of brain injuries and disease," said Christine Grady, chief of the Department of Bioethics at the NIH Clinical Center.

"It's also our duty to work with researchers to thoughtfully and proactively navigate any potential ethical issues they may encounter as they open new frontiers in brain science," she said.[3]

By contrast, in the Eastern Hemisphere, where suffering is often associated with life in the natural world, being reborn is generally seen as bad. Consequently, many Eastern religions' focus is to guide their followers in a manner to avoid returning to the physical or natural world.

The religions that hold this belief—either entirely or a subset of its followers—are Chinese Traditional (Taoism—absent the Buddhist influence), Primal-Indigenous, African Traditional & Diasporic, and Tenrikyo (see appendix B) with about 42 million followers representing 0.52 percent of the world's population. The number of Chinese Traditional (Taoism—absent the Buddhist influence) adherents with this view are not included in the above figures but would not have a material impact on the group's total.

3. Hathaway, "Scientists Restore Some Functions."

In Tenrikyo, there is one exception for the founder of the religion, Nakayama Miki—also referred to as Oyasama by some followers. Her status is special. She is considered to be "everliving." In addition, there is no conclusive evidence that followers of Tenrikyo believe the cycle of birth, death, and rebirth will ever end. However, the religion does maintain that at the conclusion of the existing creation—with a healthy dose of ambiguity about when that will be—all humans (souls) will receive salvation.

Setting aside—at this time—Tenrikyo's position that all souls will be granted salvation in the end, if this were the reality of what awaits us after death, then it makes no difference how we live our lives while on earth. Neither our actions/deeds (whether good or bad/evil) nor our beliefs (whether religious or nonreligious) during our lifetime, will be able to stop the cycle. They will have no bearing on our afterlife. Indeed, in this scenario, the term afterlife has no real meaning, because no such place or state exists. We won't explore where a soul might be as it awaits its next rebirth after death. Whatever the location or the amount of time a soul stays there, it would only be temporary. We also don't consider if the soul is in a pleasant environment or one of distress. These things may certainly be of interest but irrelevant to our discussion. Our objective lies only in understanding the final fate of the soul, which is to be reborn forever.

There is no reward for being a good person, and no punishment for being a bad person—ignoring the potential of any temporary conditions or circumstances between incarnations. Whether your achievements in your current life transfer into your next life is not a factor. We are only considering the final fate of the soul and not the "status" of a soul upon its rebirth. How much or how little we accomplished on earth in our previous life would be of no value to us. Now of course, you may experience a "better" existence in your current life if you are able to gain knowledge, wealth, fame, etc. But even here you need to be careful with this hypothesis. Better is highly subjective. One man's joy can be another man's sorrow. Likewise, one woman's junk is another woman's jewel. And of course, the Beatles made us all aware that money *Can't Buy Me Love*, or happiness.

There would be no value to an individual becoming enlightened. An enlightened person would still be powerless to stop the cycle. She would presumably be aware that her soul will be reborn after death, and then upon her death realize the same fate as everyone else who was not enlightened. God's grace, if such a being existed, would not end the cycle. In this afterlife reality, there is no distinction between a good afterlife and a bad afterlife. It depends on your perspective. As mentioned before, people in the Western Hemisphere generally view being reborn as good. People in the Eastern Hemisphere generally view it as bad. In either case, regardless of your perspective on its goodness or badness, every human would be destined to have the same fate—no exiting this world.

Reunited, and It Feels So Good

In the second outcome, the cycle of birth, death, and rebirth does come to an end. It stops when the soul reaches a good place, a good state, or a reunion with God—covering all concepts of God. It embraces Brahman, the Supreme Being, the All That Is, kami, or any other notion of a universal God, spirit, energy, or force of nature. The religions that hold this belief—either entirely or a significant number of its followers—are Hinduism, Buddhism (encompassing Taoism, Shinto, and Cao Dai), Primal-Indigenous, Sikhism, Spiritism, Jainism, Neopaganism, Unitarian Universalism, and Scientology (see appendix B). The group has a total of 1.807 billion adherents equating to 22.28 percent of the world's population.

This outcome also covers some followers of Tenrikyo. Discussed in the previous outcome, Ain't No Stopping Us Now, they maintain that all souls will receive salvation at the end of the existing creation. The number of Tenrikyo adherents with this view are not included in the above figures but would not have a material impact on the group's total.

In this afterlife reality—excluding Jainism and Shinto—all souls eventually reach the same destination. They gather in the good place, state, or reunion, often referred to as nirvana or moksha. If a human being does not reach this destination in his current lifetime, he will simply be reborn until he does. There is no limit to the number of times a soul is reborn. Sikhism teaches that there are 8.4 million species in the world, however, recent estimates place the number slightly higher.[4]

Whatever quantity is used as the exact number of species, the religion advocates that a soul will cycle through all species indefinitely until it is liberated.[5]

4. "To date, a total of 1.3 million species have been identified and described, but the truth is that many more live on Earth. The most accurate census, conducted by the Hawaii's University, estimates that a total of 8.7 million species live on the planet." Camps, "How Many Species."

5. Guru Granth Sahib Ji, 70, available online at http://www.realsikhism.com/gurbani/

Gambling With Your Soul

Therefore, no soul will ever end up in the bad place. And in most of the religions that hold this belief there is no such place. If there is a "bad" place, it is usually considered to be the physical or natural world in which we live where there is suffering, which is bad.

Like Sikhism, Jainism also teaches that each soul (with the closest Jain word being jiva, which means a conscious, living being) goes through 8.4 million—or 8.7 million if we use the most recent estimate—rebirths. The figure is most likely aligned with the number of species the religion considers to be on the planet.

However, unlike Sikhism, Jainism asserts that some souls can never attain liberation or moksha. This could be due to various reasons. It's generally the result of evil acts that have been committed. And while Sikhs believe all souls will eventually achieve liberation, the religion acknowledges that if a person does not perform righteous deeds, his soul will stay in this endless loop. For these souls, they will continue in the cycle of birth, death, and rebirth forever. Their fate is included in the previously discussed afterlife reality—The Merry-Go-Round: Ain't No Stopping Us Now.

In Shinto—absent the influence of Buddhism—the reunion of the human spirit/soul with the universal and eternal spirit (kami) is slightly different from the reunion envisioned by other religions in this group. Shinto has no concept of an eternal human spirit/soul. The spirit/soul also does not cycle through birth, death, and rebirth. Upon death, the person's spiritual energy—referred to as the soul in many religions—rejoins with kami. Kami is neither categorically good nor bad. It is simply the spiritual energy that resides in all living, and in some cases, nonliving things. Kami is capable of actions and activities that could be considered good or bad. For example, rain to a farmer experiencing a drought can be a welcomed sight—something very good. The same rain to a family at the base of a mountain facing a mudslide would be an unwelcome potential disaster—something very bad. Since that part of a human being which survives death—irrespective of its name: soul, spirit, energy, force, consciousness, etc.—reunites with a universal and eternal Spirit/Energy, Shinto is appropriately included within this afterlife reality.

While Buddhism is also included in this afterlife reality, there are some unique aspects of the religion worth noting. At its foundation, Buddhism has a similar concept of God—kami—as Shinto. However, unlike

popup.php?pagenumber=70_1.

Shinto, rebirth is a key component of Buddhism. Rebirth occurs due to karma generated in the individual's current or previous lives.

Another distinguishing feature of Buddhism—with similarities to Shinto—is the doctrine of Anatta ("Non-Self"). It is regarded as one of the seven beneficial perceptions, and one of the three marks of existence. "According to the anatta doctrine of Buddhism, at the core of all human beings and living creatures, there is no 'eternal, essential and absolute something called a soul, self or atman.' Buddhism, from its earliest days, has denied the existence of the 'self, soul' in its core philosophical and ontological texts."[6] Although absent a "personal" soul, Buddhism acknowledges that the essence—think of it as an energy—within a human being does survive physical death. And this essence or energy will continue to be reborn (or attached to a new host body) until it is liberated and unites or reunites with the one eternal God/Spirit/Energy.

In some religions (Hinduism, Buddhism, Sikhism, Spiritism, and Jainism), the soul of a person who had committed evil acts will be sent to a bad place. Their stay is temporary until the soul is cleansed of or punished for the evil deeds or bad karma it has generated. The soul may be sent there in a natural cause and effect progression under its own power, or as a deliberate judgment by another being. In Hindu that being would be Yama, the God of death, and the place is Naraka. Chinese Buddhism refers to the place as Diyu, with ten courts and multiple layers or stages. It is also presided over by the Hindu God Yama in Chinese mythology. Afterward, the soul is reborn into the physical world. It continues in the cycle to death and then rebirth until it reaches nirvana, moksha, or a similar place/state.

Naturally it may take some souls longer than others to reach this pure state and therefore, have more experiences along their journey. Some of the experiences could be exceedingly good. Others could be exceedingly bad. All rebirths may not be onto plant earth or into a human body.

For instance, Buddhism identifies six possible realms in which a soul can exist: Gods, Demi-god, Human, Animal, Hungry Ghost, and Hell.[7] The soul may or may not have an actual physical body depending on the realm. In its next life, a soul may find itself on the Moon, Jupiter, or some unknown celestial body.

The number of rebirths, locations within or outside the universe, and types of bodies that housed the soul is not a factor. It's reasonable to assume

6. *Wikipedia*, s.v. "Anattā," 6. A Difference between Buddhism and Hinduism.
7. *Wikipedia*, s.v. "Saṃsā ra (Buddhism)."

that all experiences along the way were necessary. They allowed the soul to reach maturity or enlightenment, then liberation, then nirvana, moksha, or a similar place/state. These existences were momentary stops along the highway leading to a permanent destination, which is our only concern. All religions within this group, except Spiritism and Scientology, teach that a person must rid himself of all karma—but at the very least, bad karma—to end the cycle.

The National Spiritualist Association of Churches does not espouse a belief of rebirth into the physical world. Spiritualists believe that upon death, the soul enters the spirit world. It lands at a level or realm based on the person's thoughts and actions during her lifetime on earth. The higher the realm, the better the surroundings and conditions. Lower realms can have very unpleasant conditions. Once in the spirit world, the soul will continue its progression upward within the realms—believed to be at least seven for humans—towards the Realms of the Light. Its level of attainment will depend on the soul's spiritual maturity or purity. Most souls will eventually reach the highest possible realm. However, any level above the second Realm of Light is considered good. And no soul is expected to end its progression at the first or second realm. Therefore, ending one's progression below the highest possible realm (i.e., anywhere between three and seven) results in a good afterlife. Although the soul's progression is in the spirit world, Spiritism is appropriately included within this afterlife outcome. The soul departs the merry-go-round and ultimately ends the cycle in a good place. The potential to progress to higher levels of goodness within the spirit world is a bonus.

The other religion which has a different approach to ending the cycle is Scientology. Scientology teaches that a soul, referred to as the thetan, must rid itself of psychic scars. The scars could have been inflicted over many lifetimes. The process to eliminate the scars is known as auditing. The auditor takes an individual, known as a PC or "preclear," through times in their life and claims to get rid of any past or current negative situations that may have hold on to them. Once the scars are removed, the thetan is declared "clear." Cleared thetans then progress in spiritual maturity where they eventually become pure energy. Thus, ending the cycle of death, birth, and rebirth in a good state. A thetan will continue in the cycle indefinitely until this occurs. As a result, Scientology is most appropriately included within this afterlife reality.

The group's remaining religions (Hinduism, Buddhism—encompass-ing Taoism, Shinto, and Cao Dai, Primal-Indigenous, Sikhism, Jainism,

Neopaganism, and Unitarian Universalism) focus on eliminating karma to end the cycle. There are various methods or paths to achieve the goal (see Hinduism and Buddhism in appendix B). As might be expected, the adherents from this group of religions believe that a follower of their specific religion will more easily and quickly reach this state. But nevertheless, they all assert that every human being will eventually reach this state once they stop generating karma. This becomes easier with each rebirth—so the theory goes.

The religions advocate that a soul continues its journey toward nirvana, moksha, or Sach Khand (The Realm of Truth) taking the lessons learned from the current life into the next one. Within some of these religions, for example Mahayana Buddhism and Neopaganism, the notion that a soul could continue its journey within the spiritual realm rather than the physical world is also taught.

The progression could take place in pleasant surroundings, often associated with the concept of heaven. Or it could be in a darker place, often associated with the concept of hell. The soul's journey is not dependent on the person's religious or nonreligious beliefs, but instead on his intentions, thoughts, words, and actions and resultant karma. His cumulative behaviors are driven by the lessons learned in previous lifetimes. One could be a Buddhist in this lifetime, a Christian in the next, an Atheist in the following, and a Muslim in yet another. The soul simply continues its pursuit of ridding itself of karma whether in the physical world or the spiritual realm. If there is any punishment for bad karma or misdeeds from a previous lifetime, it is only temporary.

If this were the reality of what awaits us after death, then it matters to a small degree how we live our lives. Our actions/deeds could have an impact on our next life, but not on our final or permanent afterlife.

In some instances, bad or evil deeds are punished for a specific amount of time. The soul then reenters the cycle of birth, death, and rebirth where it continues its journey. Always striving for enlightenment that leads to liberation then nirvana, moksha, or a similar condition. In other cases, there is no punishment of any kind. If the individual has not been liberated, she is simply reborn.

If bad or evil acts cause a soul to remain in a low position on the path to enlightenment, then limiting the number of bad or evil deeds would be rewarded by allowing the soul to reach the desired state sooner. It could avoid rebirth and go to the good place, state, or reunion faster. If bad or evil acts do not affect a soul's position on the path to enlightenment, then how we behave on earth in our current life would have no significance—as it relates to ending the cycle. As discussed earlier, it's a matter of personal perspective whether being reborn into the physical world is a good or bad thing.

Some religions argue that the soul continues its journey to enlightenment where it left off during its most recent life—after accounting for all merit personally gained or transferred to it. Others believe that the soul begins its journey anew with each life. Either way is acceptable. This is not a pertinent factor since we are concerned only with the soul's final fate and not how long it may take a soul to get there.

Another aspect of this afterlife reality we do not explore is the experiences a soul may have after death and before its next rebirth. As would be expected, there are numerous theories advanced by the religions that support the concept of rebirth.

Arguably one of the most detailed descriptions of the after-death experience in world literature is found in the Buddhist's text, *The Tibetan Book of the Dead*. The text outlines the soul's journey from death to rebirth, which includes an intermediate state that can last up to forty-nine days. During this forty-nine-day period, the soul—with the closest equivalent in Buddhism being consciousness—has several encounters. Some of these encounters can involve frightening apparitions. How the soul responds to these situations will determine if it achieves liberation, and be freed from the cycle of birth, death, and rebirth, or stay on the merry-go-round and reenter the birth canal. Here again either path is inconsequential. We are concerned only with the soul's final fate, which will eventually be liberation and going to a good place, a good state, or a reunion with God.

Of even less importance than our actions/deeds, will be our beliefs (whether religious or nonreligious) during our lifetime. Now clearly there is a connection between one's beliefs and one's intentions, thoughts, and resulting actions. Suppose you believe the pot in the oven is hot, and you want to avoid being burned—your intent. If you think oven mitts will help you achieve your intent, then you would put on oven mitts—your action— before removing the pot from the oven. The action you took was based on your belief, but the reward you received—not getting burned—was due solely to your intent, thought and then action of wearing the mittens. The same applies for your religious or nonreligious beliefs. Regardless of the beliefs associated with your religion or nonreligion, only your behaviors (thoughts, words, and actions), driven by your intentions, generate karma.

And in some Hindu and Buddhist traditions, even intentions or the desire for results—without subsequent actions—generate karma. Karma is either positive (good) or negative (bad). The only thing that matters is ridding yourself of karma—especially bad karma, which eventually all humans will do in this afterlife reality.

Furthermore, generating bad karma, which is the result of evil intentions, thoughts, words, or actions, is not unique to followers of any specific religion or nonreligion. All humans have equal capacity in this regard. It's reflected in the diversity of religions and nonreligions represented by individuals within the criminal justice systems throughout the world (see appendix D).

In this afterlife reality, there is no permanent bad afterlife. Therefore, every human (soul), regardless the length of time or number of rebirths, will most assuredly attain a good afterlife.

Eraser

In the third outcome, the soul will depart the merry-go-round. It is provided with a limited number of attempts to end the cycle through its own efforts. If the soul does not reach the good place, state, or reunion, it is destroyed by its creator or it simply vanishes. The Yarsan (within the Primal-Indigenous religion) holds this belief. With an estimated 2 to 3 million[8] followers, they represent 0.04 percent of the world's population. Their assertion is that the soul has 1,001 rebirths to reach the good place (referred to as Paradise by the Yarsan), state, or reunion.[9]

In this afterlife reality, the soul has either reached the good place, state, or reunion, or it has been extinguished. If extinguished, it could have been by a higher being or simply vanished under its own power. If it is in the good place, state, or reunion with God, it is of course experiencing a good afterlife. If it has been extinguished or vanished, one might conclude this outcome has resulted in a bad afterlife. However, that is not the case. For this soul it would be the same as if the soul is mortal.

Now the soul would miss out on experiencing the goodness of heaven/ Paradise, some other blissful/peaceful state, or the reunion with God. But since the soul no longer exists, it would not know that or be able to appreciate or comprehend what it is missing out on. It could not be viewed

8. *Wikipedia*, s.v. "Yarsanism."
9. Hosseini, "Life after Death."

as a punishment or undesirable condition by the soul. There would be no entity to accept the punishment or experience any harsh conditions. Once the soul disappeared, there would be nothing to have a memory or association of any kind with its former existence. It would be as if the soul was never created. Therefore, if the soul was never created, it could not have a good or bad—recall our definitions of good and bad at the beginning of this chapter—afterlife. In fact, it would have no afterlife or any other type of existence to enjoy or regret.

If this were the reality of what awaits us after death, then it matters not how we live our lives while on earth. If we can rid ourselves of karma, elevate our minds to a higher consciousness, purify our souls, or receive a God's grace then we will enjoy pleasant surroundings or dwell in the oneness with God for eternity. If we are not successful in this endeavor, then we (our souls) simply fade away with no lingering effects from our prior existence. There is no punishment and no bad place. In effect, either scenario results in a good afterlife for every human. The absence of an afterlife cannot be considered a bad afterlife for the reasons discussed above.

Judgment Day

The next afterlife possibility introduces the act of a final judgment. According to the religions that incorporate this belief into their theology, the judgment will be carried out in one of three ways:

1. The individual will be judged by her own thoughts, words, and deeds.

2. The individual will be judged by God, who is given many names: Exalted One and El Shaddai (Christianity), Allah (Islam), Jehovah and Yahweh (Judaism), Olorun (African Traditional & Diasporic), and many others.

3. The individual will be judged by Jesus Christ or by God through Jesus Christ.

In this afterlife, excluding Rastafarianism and some Primal-Indigenous religions, the soul is not reborn into the physical or natural world. You live once, you die, and then you are judged. No second chance. No do over.

Rastafarians (also referred to as Rastas) have a slight twist on this belief by incorporating the concept of reincarnation into their theology. They do believe in a single Day of Judgment, which is why they are included within this perspective of the afterlife. But until that day, all souls are re-born into the physical or natural world. Rebirth occurs immediately after death. Rastafarianism does not support the idea of any other worlds besides the physical or natural world. As such, Rastas maintain that heaven is liter-ally on earth and identified, in general, as the continent of Africa and more specifically the country of Ethiopia.

All good or righteous souls will spend eternity in heaven (also called Jannah, Gan Eden, Orun Rere, and other names). For bad or unrighteous souls, there are three possible outcomes:

1. The soul is cleansed or purified, then enters heaven for eternity.

2. The soul is destroyed or extinguished.

3. The soul spends eternity in hell (also called Jahannam, Gehinnom, Orun Buru, and other names).

Some religions assert that the degree of reward a soul will receive in heaven or the degree of punishment in hell could vary. However, since there is universal agreement that heaven is a good place and hell is a bad place, we will not explore the degrees of goodness or badness within each place. Again, our focus is only to determine the soul's final resting place or state and not the shades of grey within the location/destination.

The good place could be one distinct location, an infinite number of places, or as many locations as there are human souls. In other words, each person or soul could have their very own unique good place. And the same could hold true for the bad place.

The religions that believe in a final judgment—either entirely or a sig-nificant number of its followers—are Christianity, Islam, Primal-Indigenous, African Traditional & Diasporic, Judaism, Bahá'í, Zoroastrianism, Unitarian Universalism, and Rastafarianism (see appendix B). This group has 4.357 billion followers representing 53.72 percent of the world's population.

Control

As we turn to the three ways the judgment could be administered, the first way advocates that the soul will be judged by the individual. It will be based on her own thoughts, words, and deeds. This ideology is found within the Bahá'í religion.

In the Bahá'í faith, there is no external being that decides the soul's fate, but only what the person thought, said, and did while on earth. Based on these actions, the individual would develop a set of spiritual attributes: kindness, generosity, integrity, truthfulness, humility, and selfless service to others. These attributes or virtues will bolster her soul in the next life, which is purely spiritual.

The goal is to acquire as many spiritual attributes or virtues as possible. This will allow the soul to progress faster and from a higher level within the spirit world. Its destination is a spiritual purity that brings it close to God. It is this closeness to God that Bahá'ís refer to as heaven or paradise. Failure to develop the necessary attributes or virtues results in being apart or far from God. This state is considered hell.

Souls in the Bahá'í hell do not experience any deliberate torture or punishment inflicted by an external entity. Being apart or far from God and missing out on the bliss of this closeness is considered punishment enough.

Once in the spirit world, the soul begins its eternal progression toward God. The journey begins from the appropriate level its spiritual attributes or virtues dictated. There is no conclusive evidence that Baha'is believe every soul will attain the heaven-equivalent closeness to God. On one hand, *Wikipedia* indicates that "the Bahá'í writings state that the soul is immortal and after death it will continue to progress until it attains God's presence." On the other hand, the online encyclopedia acknowledges that "sociologist researchers have observed that Bahá'ís have an inclusivistic belief that although it may take work, most [but not all] people will eventually be saved or get to heaven."[10]

If this were the reality of what awaits us after death, then it matters to some degree how we live our lives while on earth. Our thoughts, words, and deeds will have an impact on our starting position in the next spiritual life, but not our ending position. Of lesser importance, is our beliefs (whether religious or nonreligious) during our lifetime. What really matters is accumulating as many spiritual attributes or virtues as possible. This will enhance our starting point within the afterlife. There is no evidence to suggest that followers of any specific belief system will be the most successful in this pursuit. All humans have equal capacity in this regard.

In this afterlife reality, failure to achieve a closeness with God results in a bad afterlife. Every human has the same opportunity and equal probability of achieving this closeness and a good afterlife. The initial level from

10. *Wikipedia*, s.v. "Bahá'í View on Death."

which they start their progression in the spirit world does not matter. As the English poet William Ernest Henley wrote and the award-winning actor Morgan Freeman so eloquently spoke in the film *Invictus*, "I am the master of my fate: I am the captain of my soul."

The Scales of Justice

In the second way the judgment is carried out, the individual will be judged by God. The religions that subscribe to this ideology are Islam, African Traditional & Diasporic, Judaism, Zoroastrianism, Unitarian Universalism, and Rastafarianism.

The judgment is predicated on the individual's foundational belief in God, that he, she, or it does indeed exist and will exercise judgment on all souls. A person who does not believe in a God that passes judgment is viewed as not fearing or said another way, not respecting God, shunning God, or turning away from righteousness. Without this belief, the person's soul will be sent to hell, irrespective of their deeds.

The criteria or yardstick God will use varies among these religions. In general, it will be a balancing or weighing of good deeds or righteous acts against bad/evil deeds or unrighteous acts. If your good deeds outweigh your bad deeds, you go to heaven. If your bad deeds outweigh your good deeds, you go to hell.

Within some of the religions, there is an intermediate or in-between place if your good and bad/evil deeds are weighed equally. It can also be the place where the soul goes to be purified or punished for its bad/evil deeds. In the Christian Roman Catholic denomination this place is known as Purgatory and as Sheol or Gehinnom in some Jewish traditions.

All religions that believe in such a place advocate that the soul's tenure is only temporary in this location. Once the soul is cleansed of its bad/evil deeds or the soul is credited with enough additional good deeds to tip the scales, it then proceeds to heaven for the rest of eternity. A soul can acquire the additional good deeds through numerous methods. According to Catholics, a soul can gain merit from another individual's abundance of good deeds or from prayers by those still alive. Other religions promote different approaches, culminating in the same outcome. The soul eventually goes to heaven.

Islam teaches that in addition to your deeds, God will also judge your intentions. If you meant to do good, but the actual result turned out to be bad/evil, you will be given some credit in the good column. On the flip side, if you planned to do something bad/evil, but did not actually carry it out, you get hit with the consequences of that bad/evil intention.

Zoroastrianism teaches that, along with your deeds (physical actions/activities), you will be judged based on your words and thoughts during your lifetime.

Judaism teaches that God will place human beings into two groups before passing judgment: Jews and Non-Jews (Gentiles). Jewish people are thought to have a reserved place in heaven (called Gan Eden in Judaism) within Olam ha-bah (the World to Come) based on their study of Torah along with prayer, adherence to the six hundred and thirteen Commandments as applicable to the individual, repentance, and overall good deeds. However, their reservation can be cancelled due to sins.

Righteous Gentiles are eligible to receive salvation based on whether they have fulfilled seven commandments believed to be from God, although they are not explicitly stated in the Torah:

1. Establish courts of justice

2. Refrain from blaspheming the God of Israel

3. Do not engage in idolatry

4. Avoid sexual perversion

5. Refrain from bloodshed

6. Do not commit robbery

7. Do not eat meat cut from a living animal[11]

If this were the reality of what awaits us after death, then it most definitely matters how we live our lives while on earth. Our beliefs, actions/deeds (including words and thoughts), and intentions (per Islam) become extremely important. They will determine our soul's destination. All good souls of course go to heaven for eternity. To have qualified as a good soul, your good deeds and righteous behavior would have outweighed your bad deeds and unrighteous behavior.

Using the yardstick suggested by Islam, in addition to the good deeds, your intentions would have also been included in balancing the scale. With your intentions piled on, the scale would have tipped in the direction of goodness.

---

11. *Patheos,* "Judaism," §Beliefs: Afterlife and Salvation.

According to the requirements laid out by Judaism, a Jew's study of Torah, prayer, observance of the applicable six hundred and thirteen Commandments, repentance, and good deeds would have been found acceptable. The non-Jew (Gentile) would have fulfilled the seven commandments and found to be good, righteous, and acceptable. These seven commandments, except the first one, are actions an individual would personally engage in or avoid. Passing judgment on whether a person achieved them is straightforward. It is not clear how God will determine if the individual fulfilled the first commandment: establish courts of justice.

The establishment of courts of justice would likely be accomplished by a group of individuals on behalf of a larger population. If you were part of the group that set up the courts of justice, then your assessment would be straightforward. However, if you were not personally involved in this activity, Judaism does not provide an explanation of how the judgment of this specific commandment will be carried out.

To determine a bad soul's final resting place, we need to revisit the three potential outcomes postulated by the religions that subscribe to the belief of a final judgment. Again, this only applies to individuals who believed in the existence of a God who will pass judgment on souls while they were alive on earth. Those who did not are sent straight to hell, where their soul could be tormented for all eternity.

Purified

In the first potential outcome, the bad soul is purified, then sent to heaven for eternity. There is no consensus on where the soul's purification takes place (hell, purgatory, the Bardo, or some other locale) or how long the purification process takes (a day, a month, a year, or a million years). However, since we are only interested in the final fate of the soul, all opinions are acceptable rendering these questions insignificant and irrelevant to our discussion.

If this were the reality of the Judgment Day afterlife, then it makes no difference how we live our lives while on earth—provided we believe in a God that will pass judgment on all souls. Neither our actions/deeds nor intentions (whether good or bad/evil) during our lifetime, will determine our final resting place. It wouldn't matter if we were a Jew or non-Jew, and whether we met the requirements to study Torah, pray, adhere to the applicable six hundred and thirteen Commandments, repent, do good, or fulfill the seven commandments.

There is no reward—except getting to heaven sooner—for being a good person and no permanent punishment for being a bad person. Again, we are only considering the final fate of the soul and not what a soul may endure before arriving at its ultimate destination, where it will spend eternity. How much or how little we accomplish on earth would be of no consequence to us. There would be no value to an individual becoming enlightened. The person would presumably be aware that their soul will ultimately end up in heaven, and then upon his death enjoy the same fate as everyone else who was not enlightened. In this afterlife reality, every soul that believed in a God that passes judgment enjoys a good afterlife.

Destroyed

In the second potential outcome, the bad soul is destroyed or extinguished. At first glance, it appears this outcome would result in a bad afterlife for some souls even if they believed in a judging God. However, upon closer examination, that is not the case. For these souls it would be the same as if the soul is not immortal.

Now the soul would of course miss out on experiencing the goodness of heaven. But since the soul no longer exists, it would not know that or be able to appreciate or comprehend what it is missing out on. It could not be viewed as an undesirable condition by the soul since there would be nothing or no one to accept the punishment. Once the soul was destroyed, it would have no memory or association of any kind with its former existence. It would be as if the soul was never created. Now if the soul was never created, it could not have a good or bad—recall our definitions of good and bad at the beginning of this chapter—afterlife. In fact, it would have no afterlife or any other type of existence to enjoy or regret.

Therefore, this outcome also results in the equivalent of a good afterlife for every soul that believed in a judging God. No afterlife is not the same as a bad afterlife for the reasons stated above.

Punished

In the third potential outcome, the bad soul is sent to hell for a horrible and undesirable eternal existence.

If this were the reality of the Judgment Day afterlife, then it absolutely matters how we live our lives while on earth. Even if we believed in a God who passes judgment, our deeds—encompassing words, thoughts, and actions—and intentions (per Islam) will seal our fate. A good afterlife is not assured for every person.

The Lion and the Lamb

We conclude our discussion of the ways the judgment could be administered with the third way. Here the individual will be judged by Jesus Christ or by God through Jesus Christ. The only religion that subscribes to this ideology is Christianity (including individuals of other faiths who have accepted Christian beliefs, but identify with another faith; so, they are effectively Christians).

Christians believe that our path to a good afterlife goes through Jesus Christ. It is not based on a judgment or balancing of our deeds (encompassing words, thoughts, and actions) or intentions. The criteria Jesus will use hinges on our belief about who he is. In Matthew 16:13–17 (New International Version), Jesus asks his disciples, "Who do people say the Son of Man is?" They replied, "Some say John the Baptist; others say Elijah; and still others, Jeremiah or one of the prophets." "But what about you?" he asked. "Who do you say I am?" Simon Peter answered, "You are the Christ, the Son of the living God." Jesus goes on to say, "Blessed are you, Simon son of Jonah, for this was not revealed to you by man, but by my Father in heaven."

Believing that Jesus Christ is the Son of God is a foundational requirement, but Christianity also teaches that you must act on this belief. The most important acts are described in Romans 10:9 (New International Version), which states that "if you confess with your mouth, 'Jesus is Lord,' and believe in your heart that God raised him from the dead, you will be saved."

Let me pause here for a minute to reflect on the phasing in this statement around the word believe. What does it mean to "believe in your heart"? What if you only believe in your mind but not in your heart? You know. The kind of pseudo belief that doesn't have any actions behind it. That's not the kind of belief referred to here—or for that matter, anywhere else in this book. Your belief must be genuine, where you absolutely think—and feel— your belief is the truth. A Google search returns the following definition: "accept (something) as true; feel sure of the truth of."

Having your belief confirmed as the truth is not the requirement. But only that you think it is true, and act in accordance with that belief. Go back to the case of the dichromat. You will recall that in this instance he was wrong. The light for him was red. However, he truly believed it was green. Therefore, he proceeded through the light. If he thought the light was green but stopped his vehicle—as if the light was red—one would question if he truly believed the light was green. His actions would not have been consistent with his beliefs. Now this is not to suggest that individuals' actions always align perfectly with their beliefs. Attempting to understand the reasons why this occurs is beyond the scope of this book. Furthermore, determining whether the belief an individual professes is truly in his heart is beyond the ability of human beings. That's between the person and God—if he, she, or it exists.

Now let's get back to this final Judgment Day scenario.

The Christian Holy Scriptures further document how the judgment will be carried out for an individual who has not completed these acts. In Matthew 10:32–33 (New International Version), Jesus states, "Whoever acknowledges me before men, I will also acknowledge him before my Father in heaven. But whoever disowns me before men, I will disown him before my Father in heaven."

And finally, the Christian bible asserts that there is no other way to God except through Jesus Christ. In John 14:6 (New International Version), when questioned about the place he was preparing for his followers and how to get there, Jesus answered his disciple Thomas by saying, "I am the way and the truth and the life. No one comes to the Father except through me."

If this were the reality of the Judgment Day afterlife, then how we live our lives while on earth most certainly matters. In addition to a belief in a judging God, we must verbally acknowledge that Jesus Christ is Lord—The Son of God—and believe in our heart that God raised him from the dead to be the Savior of the world. Only by completing these acts can we gain admittance into heaven and enjoy a good afterlife. Failure to meet these foundational requirements will cause us to be sentenced to hell for all eternity. Christianity is the only religion that holds to this teaching. Therefore, in this afterlife reality, it is clear all humans will not have the same fate. Only Christians will go to the good place (heaven). All others will go to the bad place (hell) for all eternity.

Decision Day

Another afterlife possibility we consider is not one that is advocated by any of the religions discussed in this book—with one possible exception being Juche, which advocates that man is the master of everything and decides everything; so, whatever happens after death will be decided by man. It has no official following and does not receive serious debate among religious scholars. However, it has garnered the attention of many Gen-X, Millennial, and Generation Z individuals. At the heart of this afterlife possibility is the belief that the individual creates her own reality—in life and in death.

If indeed this could be achieved, it would mean that each person decides their afterlife fate. Either prior to or after death, the person would choose the type of afterlife they would enjoy. The ability to choose is not granted because of how we lived our lives while on earth. The decision point is not taken away based on our actions/deeds, whether good or bad. We also do not lose the ability to choose due to our beliefs, ideologies, self-awareness, or level of spiritual awakening. These things simply have no bearing on the option we have been granted.

If this were the reality of what awaits us after death, then clearly it does not matter how we live our lives while on earth. Neither our actions/deeds—including intentions (whether good or bad/evil) nor our beliefs (whether religious or nonreligious) during our lifetime, will have any bearing on our afterlife. Now these things could have an impact on our choice, so in that sense, they will affect our afterlife. Perhaps the person's experiences while alive on earth will play a role in their decision regarding their afterlife. That possibility is beyond this discussion. The fact that we would have an opportunity to make a thoughtful choice trumps all previous actions, deeds, beliefs, or intentions.

There is no reward for being a good person and no punishment for being a bad person, unless that is what we desired. And if that was indeed our desire, then the punishment could not be considered bad since it was our choice. How much or how little we accomplish on earth would be of no importance. There would be no benefit to an individual becoming enlightened. The person would presumably be aware that their soul will spend eternity based on their individual decision. Then upon death, they would experience the results of their choice like everyone else who was not enlightened. God's grace, if such a being existed, would be offered to everyone—whether the person believed in God's existence or not—equally in granting each soul the opportunity to choose.

In this afterlife reality, we cannot distinguish between a good afterlife and a bad afterlife. It depends on each person's individual perspective. But regardless of one's perspective, every human being would have the ability to choose a good afterlife according to their desires.

Extreme Measures

The final afterlife possibility we consider has two potential alternatives. Like the Decision Day possibility, it is not explicitly advocated by any of the religions in our discussion. However, several religions do support the idea of only a good place as an ultimate destination, which aligns with the first alternative. Before arriving at its final locale, a bad soul may have a temporary stop according to some religions.

We look at the book ends of goodness and badness promoted by the religious community. This encompasses all concepts of good and bad—as defined at the beginning of this chapter. What makes this afterlife possibility different from the typical view where a soul can end up in either heaven, including a heavenly state, or hell, including a hellish state, is the fact that only one destination or state exists. Everyone shares the same fate.

Getting to this place or state is not based on what we believed, did, or intended to do while we were alive on earth. The sinner and the saint, the religious and nonreligious, the good girl and the bad boy will all spend eternity in the same place or state. And since we are only interested in the soul's final resting place or state, we will not consider the potential degrees of comfort or torment within each location. We accept that all of heaven or a heavenly state is good, and all of hell or a hellish state is bad.

If this were the reality of what awaits us after death, then it obviously does not matter how we live our lives while on earth. Neither our actions/deeds—including intentions (whether good or bad/evil) nor our beliefs (whether religious or nonreligious) during our lifetime, will have any bearing on our afterlife. Whether we proceed to the destination/state immediately after death or after being reborn for many lifetimes then proceed to that same destination/state is irrelevant. If we lived those lifetimes as a human being, animal, plant, or something else, our fate would not be altered. If we existed in the physical world on Earth, Mars, a moon, sun, or some other celestial body, or in the spiritual realm, in the end, our soul would join all other souls in the same gathering place or state.

The Hereafters

There is no reward for being a good person, and no punishment for being a bad person. How much or how little we accomplish in the physical world or spiritual world would have no significance. There would be no benefit afforded to an individual who became enlightened. The person would presumably be aware that their soul will spend eternity in either heaven or a heavenly state or in hell or a hellish state. And then upon his death proceed to that destination/state like everyone else who was not enlightened. There would be no need for and no value in receiving God's grace—if such a being existed.

In this afterlife alternative, if heaven or a heavenly state is the reality everyone will have a good afterlife. If hell or a hellish state is the reality everyone will have a bad afterlife.

Reflections

What is the purpose of your life?

What do you believe will happen to your soul when you die?

Have you or has someone you know had an encounter with a spirit (i.e., non-flesh-and-blood entity)? If so, what was the experience, and how did it impact you?

6

Place Your Bet

Gambling: The sure way of getting nothing from something.

—WILSON MIZNER

The world is like a reverse casino. In a casino, if you gamble long enough,
you're certainly going to lose. But in the real world, where the only thing
you're gambling is, say, your time or your embarrassment, then the more stuff
you do, the more you give luck a chance to find you.

—SCOTT ADAMS

Markets are constantly in a state of uncertainty and flux and money is made
by discounting the obvious and betting on the unexpected.

—GEORGE SOROS

"GAMBLING DATES BACK TO the Paleolithic period, before written history.
In Mesopotamia the earliest six-sided dice date to about 3000 BC. However,
they were based on astragali dating back thousands of years earlier. In
China, gambling houses were widespread in the first millennium BC, and
betting on fighting animals was common. Lotto games and dominoes (pre-
cursors of Pai Gow) appeared in China as early as the 10th century."[1]

1. *Wikipedia*, s.v. "Gambling," 1. History.

"Gambling (also known as betting) is the wagering of money or something of value (referred to as 'the stakes') on an event with an uncertain outcome, with the primary intent of winning money or material goods. Gambling thus requires three elements to be present: consideration (an amount wagered), risk (chance), and a prize."[2] The element of chance, or otherwise known as risk—the possibility of loss, danger, or injury—is a well understood component of a gamble. So too is prize—often described as the payout. Consideration is not.

In the context of gambling, consideration is a concept of English common law, which has also been adopted by the United States. According to the *Merriam-Webster* dictionary, "It is the inducement to a contract or other legal transaction; specifically: an act or forbearance or the promise thereof done or given by one party in return for the act or promise of another."[3] In other words, I'll pay you $10 (the prize or payout) in exchange for (or in consideration of) the $5 (the inducement to the contract—the stakes) you give to me, provided you win the bet. If you lose, I give you $0 (consequence of taking a chance—the risk) and keep the $5 (the stakes).

Risky Business

Let's explore the assertion of *Gambling With Your Soul*. First, the item being wagered (the stakes) must be something of value. Does a human soul have value?

Jesus said, "For what shall it profit a man, if he shall gain the whole world, and lose his own soul?" (Mark 8:36 King James Version). According to the International Monetary Fund (IMF), at the close of 2020, the worldwide economy totaled $87.6 trillion, with the United States and China leading all countries with $21.4 trillion and $15.2 trillion of Gross Domestic Product (GDP), respectively.[4] If the soul is worth as much as the entire world, then certainly it is a thing of value. But why would your soul have value?

If we look at a work of art, an original is worth much more than a copy. You can pick up a reproduction of Leonardo da Vinci's *Mona Lisa* on Amazon.com for about $50, while a gallery quality hand-painted oil of the masterpiece will set you back around $1,500. And the real thing will run you a cool $850 million.

2. *Wikipedia*, s.v. "Gambling."

3. *Merriam-Webster*, s.v. "Consideration."

4. *Wikipedia*, s.v. "World Economy."

Guinness World Records lists da Vinci's *Mona Lisa* as having the highest ever insurance value for a painting. On permanent display at the Louvre in Paris, the *Mona Lisa* was assessed at US$100 million on December 14, 1962. Taking inflation into account, the 1962 value would be around US$850 million in 2019. The current record price [for a painting] is approximately US$400 million paid for Leonardo da Vinci's *Salvator Mundi* in November 2017.[5]

What about the personal effects of your favorite musician? How much would a collector pay for the guitar strummed by Jimi Hendrix at Woodstock? Consider a vintage automobile like the 1968 Ford Mustang fastback driven by Steve McQueen in the classic Hollywood movie *Bullitt*. Or a one-of-a-kind Boeing VC-25A—the military version of the iconic wide-body commercial 747 aircraft—nicknamed "The Queen of the Skies" and better known as Air Force One when the president of the United States is on board.

According to the economic concept of supply and demand, the more limited the supply, the greater the value of the item being sought. And what is more limited than your very soul? It's a one-of-a kind, an original, and it can last forever. It is quite literally, priceless.

To clear the next hurdle in satisfying the requirement of a gamble, the event must have an uncertain outcome. In the case of gambling with your soul, the event is death—of the human being—itself, or more precisely, what comes after death. Fulfilling this requirement is accomplished by accepting fundamental truth #2: No one knows what will happen to you when you die. Therefore, the outcome is surely uncertain.

To satisfy the final criteria of a gamble, there must be an intent of winning a prize or being awarded something of value. While the usual reward in a gamble is money or material goods, it need not be. For example, fame, status, or an exceptional experience are all legitimate payouts for a gamble, provided the individual placing the bet finds value in them. In the case of gambling with your soul, the intent is to win or be awarded a good afterlife. This is both desirable and valuable to all human beings. Therefore, wagering your soul for the chance of a good afterlife meets all the requirements to be a gamble.

This is the specific bet we each make: An external being, typically thought of as God, will give my soul a good afterlife (the prize or payout) in exchange for (or in consideration of) my choice to live life in accordance

---

5. *Wikipedia*, s.v. "Most Expensive Paintings."

with its desires. If the external being does exist, and I choose not to live my life in accordance with its desires, my soul (the stakes) will receive a bad afterlife (consequences of taking a chance—the risk). If the external being does not exist, then the bet is void. It's as if the wager was never made. There is no prize or payout, but also no consequences. The stakes (my soul) are returned to me and will experience whatever comes next—if anything. In the same vein, if I don't have a soul, then the bet is also void since I would have nothing to wager or offer as the stakes. Again, there is no prize or payout, but also no consequences.

Ordinarily placing a bet is a voluntary activity. Of course, there may be a situation where a person feels compelled to place a bet. Perhaps in hopes of a big payout to meet a financial obligation. But even then, the person still makes an intentional, calculated, and deliberate decision to place the bet.

In the case of gambling with your soul, you are not afforded the opportunity to decide if you want to make a bet. With the simple event of you being born, the game is started. Is that fair? Maybe not, but it's the hand you are dealt. You cannot sit out this hand, opt out of the game, or delegate the responsibility to someone else. Choosing to have no belief regarding the afterlife—attempting to ignore the situation—does not end the game. And it's a game where taking a neutral position is not an option. Having no belief is—for all intents and purposes—the same as saying there is no afterlife. Therefore, since your only alternative is to make the bet, you might as well play to win. Given this reality, how should you live your life to give yourself the best chance of winning—being rewarded with the prize of a good afterlife?

Playing the Odds

Let's evaluate our unavoidable circumstance by considering the analysis we would employ when placing a bet. Assume that you have $100 (the stakes) to bet, and you can choose between three options upon which to place your wager. All three options provide the same payout if you are a winner. Let's say $200 (the prize). You double your money.

In option #1, you have a 25 percent chance of winning. In option #2, you have a 50 percent chance of winning. And in option #3, you have a 75 percent chance of winning. The bet will cost you the same $100 in all three options. Which option do you choose?

Naturally, you choose option #3. It would be foolish to accept a lower probability of winning (i.e., have a lower chance at getting a fixed prize— take on more risk) without also having the opportunity to receive a higher reward or payout.

Applying this logic to our topic of the afterlife, where the stakes (our soul) are the same and the payout or prize (a good afterlife) is the same, we would choose the religious or nonreligious ideology that offers the greatest chance—highest probability—of achieving a good afterlife.

You will note that in the example with the three options, we are not concerned with which option is "right." When placing a bet—which covers making an investment and executing virtually all significant business decisions—we walk through a process to answer three major questions:

1. Should I make a bet (i.e., Should I play the game)?

2. What do I bet on (i.e., What is the best option/alternative)?

3. How much should I wager (i.e., What are the stakes)?

In answering the first question, we consider all moral, ethical, strategic, and any other big picture factors. It's during this stage of the analysis where we address the question of "right" or "wrong." If the game, investment, or business proposition does not align with our values or objectives, then it's not right for us. We simply choose not to play, invest, or execute. We walk away. Once we decide to engage, we move on to the next question.

For the second question, the goal is to achieve the greatest return on our bet, investment, or business proposition while taking the least amount of risk. These choices are viewed in terms of better and worse, as opposed to right and wrong. Ultimately, the best—and therefore the "right"—bet, investment, or business decision is the one which provides the highest payout with the lowest amount of risk in relation to all other alternatives. At this stage of the analysis, the question of right or wrong is not part of the decision-making process. That was addressed with the first question. Now it's all about the math.

After determining where to place our bet, we then answer the third question by deciding how much to wager or invest.

As discussed earlier, in the case of gambling with your soul, the first question is answered with the simple event of you being born. The game is started. There is no walking away. You also do not get a choice in your response to question number 3 of how much to wager. The stakes are your soul. You're all in. The only question left for you to answer is question number 2: What do I bet on?

For many of us, being placed in these types of situations makes us uncomfortable, and that's perfectly normal.

In fact, renowned psychologist Abraham Harold Maslow has affirmed that the natural uncertainty found in these situations—where speculation is required on future events with incomplete, possibly inaccurate, and often conflicting information—do not align well with some of our innate human needs. Specifically, Maslow theorized that all human beings have five levels—late in his life, he added a sixth level: transcendence—of needs that must be satisfied for a person to reach her full potential. He placed them in a hierarchy from the lowest to the highest, but also emphasized that the hierarchy is not a rigid fixed order as it is often presented.

- Level 1: Physical Survival Needs

- Level 2: Physical Safety Needs

- Level 3: Love and Belonging Needs

- Level 4: Self-Esteem Needs

- Level 5: Self-Fulfilled (Self-Actualized) Needs

Fulfilling the first four levels may eventually culminate in achieving Level 5: Self-Actualization. However, self-actualization is not an automatic outcome of satisfying the other four lower levels of human needs. With that said, levels 1 through 4 must be fulfilled before level 5 can be achieved. And according to Maslow, as well as Confucianism, self-actualization is the desire—either consciously or subconsciously—of every human being.

Wrapped securely within the level 4 need, is our relentless and instinctive drive to be right with the decisions we make in this life. At level 4, we find that,

> with a few exceptions, people in our society have a need to feel of value and to count for something. This is called the need for esteem. It is a degree of self-respect and respect from others. Self-respect includes the need for confidence, achievement, independence and freedom. Respect from others includes recognition, attention and appreciation.[6]

6. "Maslow's Hierarchy," www.theneurotypical.com/maslows_basic_needs.html.

All the accolades and respect from others, as well as the elements to build self-respect, are influenced by the accuracy of our decisions. When was the last time you were praised or rewarded for being wrong? Exactly.

If we could be right with every decision, or at least the major ones, that would be awesome. It would be a significant enabler to fulfill the self-esteem need identified at level 4. And according to Maslow, it may be a bona fide requirement. Maslow further asserts that we must fulfill the needs at this level to have an opportunity to reach our full potential—every human's desire. And that happens through self-actualization found at level 5.

Unfortunately, in the scenarios described above, we can't know the accuracy of our decisions. It's impossible to determine if we are making the right call when we place the bet, buy the stock, or pull the trigger to launch a new product. Deciding which religion or nonreligion to follow presents us with a similar dilemma. It is a situation where the future outcome of our decision cannot be known in advance. This puts each of us in the same boat alongside the gambler, investor, or businessperson. As the saying goes, "Hindsight is 20/20," but it's blind at the time we must make the decision.

With most actions, the outcome from our decision is realized within our lifetime. This could be almost immediately or within a few hours, days, weeks, or months. As a result, we can use the knowledge gained from the actual outcome to help with future decisions. Where we were wrong, we would learn from our mistakes and make an adjustment in our decision-making process. Allowing us to avoid another undesired result. Where we were right, we would have confirmation that our decision-making process is sound. We would continue deploying it on future decisions.

In the context of the afterlife, our task is especially daunting since we don't have the benefit of assessing the outcome of previous decisions in this area. We certainly can't evaluate our own personal decision since we have not died—as previously defined in chapter 4—and come back to life. And we also can't turn to the decisions of others for guidance.

Do we know the whereabouts of our departed loved ones? What about the individual—or more precisely, the individual's soul—who started or inspired the formation of the religion or nonreligion we have chosen to follow? Our first instinct is to answer affirmatively. Yes. Of course, I know. As human beings, we fear the unknown. To reduce that fear, we convince ourselves that we do know. However, based on our understanding of the word *know*, that's unfortunately not the truth. And that goes against everything we have been taught and most likely contradicts what we have told others. That's incredibly difficult and unsettling for us to even think about, much less accept. It evokes thoughts, feelings, and sensations that are truly frightening.

So, let's pretend for the moment that we do know. This still will not allow us to answer The Question. There is no way of knowing we will end up in the same place—assuming of course it's somewhere we want to be. And that makes this predicament different from most—if not all—other situations we face during our lifetime.

Viewing this type of situation from another perspective, let's revisit the routine of preflight planning discussed in the introduction. Suppose you are the plane's pilot. Your journey will start from Lebanon, Kansas—about two miles from the geographical center of the forty-eight contiguous United States. You will be flying to one of three cities: Dallas, Miami, or Anchorage. The plane will need to reach and sustain an altitude of either twenty or thirty-five thousand feet for 80 percent of the flight. You will be transporting either twelve or twenty-four passengers plus luggage. And you will encounter either a headwind or a tailwind of fifteen knots for the duration of the journey.

Once in flight, you will be unable to land the plane until you reach the target destination. There is no option to refuel en route, and you cannot abort the mission or return to the place of departure. How do you ensure a successful journey?

Naturally, you reason that the plane—fully fueled—would need to be capable of handling the most demanding requirement for each variable. You start with the potential destination cities and assume that Anchorage is the location. For altitude, you pick thirty-five thousand feet. There would be twenty-four passengers with luggage in your calculations. And you would factor in a headwind of fifteen knots throughout the flight.

By preparing for the most demanding condition—taking all variables into account, you are assured of a successful outcome for all conditions. In your preflight planning routine, if you determine the plane cannot achieve the mission, you hit pause. Your options: get another plane or do not embark on the journey. But, if you assumed for example, the destination city is Dallas and leave Lebanon heading north—oops.

Getting back to the specific mission at hand—achieve a good afterlife—you cannot refuse to embark on the journey. If you are reading this book, you are already in the air and heading toward the destination—at least the first known destination: physical death. Now, until you reach this first known destination or waypoint, you can change planes. You can make a midcourse correction to improve your chances of a successful mission. However, once you reach this waypoint, the ability to alter your aircraft ends. We will come back to this point a bit later in our discussion.

Employing similar logic as the above two examples, let's determine the probability of a good afterlife for followers of each religion and nonreligion based on the potential afterlife realities discussed in chapter 5. We have already stipulated that if the human soul is not immortal or if a human being does not have a soul, then what happens to it is irrelevant. Those eventualities would be considered not applicable (N/A) or in our case no afterlife (N/A). Nevertheless, they are still relevant to our discussion and subsequent analysis. As we have defined it, no afterlife is not the same as a bad afterlife. We will revisit this point later in more detail.

Birth Right

Before starting our analysis, I need to address a potential afterlife scenario which we have not discussed up to this point. It is the assertion that an individual is awarded a good afterlife based solely on their race or ethnicity, and anyone outside the race or ethnic group is doomed to have a bad afterlife. This afterlife possibility is not included. For starters, it would not satisfy the criteria of a gamble, which requires the elements of consideration, chance, and prize. Consideration and chance are not present.

In this scenario, the person is not required to make a choice or offer anything for consideration. Also, since a good afterlife would be guaranteed, there is no potential of losing something of value. This eliminates the component of chance or risk. Furthermore, every race and ethnic group can make the same claim. And since it is not possible to verify any such assertion as being true, everyone would be afforded the same probability of being correct. That would neutralize the effect on the scoring, which would have the same relative impact of not including it. To simplify the analysis, I have taken the latter approach.

Without a Trace

The first afterlife possibility to analyze, Without a Trace, is one where there is no form of life after death. This scenario is N/A. For if this is the reality of what awaits us after death, then there is no such thing as a good, but more importantly a bad, afterlife. In fact, the word afterlife would be meaningless. Now, let's look at the remaining afterlife possibilities in chapter 5.

Déjà Vu

We start with the Déjà Vu possibility where there is no heaven—in the traditional sense as a type of paradise, and no hell—in the traditional sense as a place of punishment, where God(s) may or may not exist. The environment would be very much as it is today on earth, with uncertainty and subjectivity about the goodness and badness of a soul's condition in a spiritual world. Every soul, no matter what they believed, did, or intended to do while alive, would have to learn the rules of their new spiritual world. They would determine what it takes to create a good existence for themselves. Based on their individual desire, they would align their beliefs and actions to achieve that desired state, good or bad. As it is on earth, the results will not always meet the desired intent or goal. It is just as likely that the soul will be successful in creating a good/desired outcome or condition as a bad/undesired outcome or condition. Therefore, followers of every religion and nonreligion are assigned a probably of 0.50 or 50 percent of attaining a good/desired afterlife.

The Merry-Go-Round

The next afterlife possibility we score is the Merry-Go-Round, which offers three potential outcomes.

I. Ain't No Stopping Us Now

In the first outcome there is no end to the cycle of birth, death, and rebirth into the physical or natural world. There is no other place, dimension, or state for souls apart from the physical realm in which we currently exist. Here again, the term afterlife has no relevance because there is no such thing. Therefore, like the Without a Trace possibility, it is N/A.

II. Reunited, and It Feels So Good

The second outcome concludes with all souls reaching a good place, a good state, or a reunion with God, Brahman, the Supreme Being, the All That Is, kami, the universe itself, or any other similar concept of a universal God, spirit, energy, or force of nature. There is no permanent bad place or state in this afterlife reality. Consequently, followers of every religion or nonreligion are guaranteed a good afterlife. A probability of 1.00 or 100 percent is assigned to everyone.

III. Eraser

In the third outcome each soul is afforded a limited number of rebirths. The goal is to reach a good place, a good state, or a reunion with a supreme being, spirit, energy, or force of nature and depart the merry-go-round. If the soul is unable to get there, it is destroyed by its creator or simply vanishes.

As discussed earlier, a soul that is extinguished would have no way of experiencing, remembering, enjoying, or regretting anything, good or bad. In effect, it would be the same as if the soul was never created or the soul is mortal. For our analysis, this eventuality is considered N/A for every soul. On the other hand, if the soul is successful in reaching the good place, good state, or reunion, then it of course experiences a good afterlife. Since there is no bad place or state, either eventuality in this third outcome is good. Therefore, followers of every religion or nonreligion are assigned a probability of 1.00 or 100 percent of achieving a good afterlife.

Judgment Day

We now turn to the Judgment Day afterlife possibility where the soul is subjected to a final judgment in one of three ways:

1. The individual is judged by her own thoughts, words, and deeds.
2. The individual is judged by God.
3. The individual is judged by Jesus Christ or by God through Jesus Christ.

Excluding Bahá'í, to be eligible for judgment, the person must have believed in a God who will pass judgment on human souls while she was alive. Without this fundamental belief, the soul is sent to hell. Followers of those religions or nonreligions which do not acknowledge the existence of this type of God would have no chance of attaining a good afterlife. Therefore, they have been assigned a probability of 0.00 or 0 percent for all Judgment Day possibilities except the Bahá'í scenario.

The Bahá'í religion—captured in the afterlife possibility Judgment Day: Control—teaches that a person will be judged by his own thoughts, words, and deeds. There is no external entity that decides the soul's fate, but only what the human being thought, said, and did while on earth. It does not require a belief in or acknowledgment of God, but rather an accumulation of spiritual attributes—kindness, generosity, integrity, truthfulness, humility, and selfless service to others. After death, the soul enters the spirit world with those attributes or virtues and begins its progression toward God. Achieving a closeness to God is considered heaven. Being apart from God is hell. Every soul, regardless of the person's beliefs, actions, or intentions while alive, has the same capacity of achieving this closeness. However, attaining it is not guaranteed. It is just as likely that a soul will attain this closeness as it is the soul will not. Therefore, followers of every religion and nonreligion are assigned a probably of 0.50 or 50 percent of experiencing a good afterlife.

We next look at the Judgment Day possibility (The Scales of Justice) that requires a belief in a God that will judge human souls, and the judgment will be carried out by God. Souls judged to be good are sent to heaven or its equivalent. There are three potential outcomes for a soul deemed to be bad.

I. Purified

In the first potential outcome, the bad soul is purified, then sent to heaven for eternity. The length, locale, or amount of cleansing required is not considered in the analysis since we are only concerned with the soul's final fate. Followers of every God-fearing (i.e., having a belief in the existence of a God who will pass judgment on all souls) religion are guaranteed a good afterlife. Everyone receives a probability of 1.00 or 100 percent.

II. Destroyed

The second potential outcome is analogous to the third outcome of the Merry-Go-Round: Eraser possibility. In this afterlife reality God destroys the bad soul. As discussed earlier, a soul that is destroyed would have no way of experiencing, remembering, enjoying, or regretting anything, good or bad. In effect, it would be the same as if the soul was never created or the soul is mortal. For our analysis, since there is no bad place, state, or condition, followers of every God-fearing religion are assigned a probability of 1.00 or 100 percent of achieving a good afterlife.

III. Punished

In the third potential outcome, the bad soul is sent to hell. There it would be subjected to a tormented and undesirable existence. The punishment is for all eternity. The religions that believe in such an eventuality are Islam, some African Traditional & Diasporic, and some adherents of Judaism.

The other religions—some adherents of African Traditional & Diasporic, Primal-Indigenous, Judaism, and Unitarian Universalism, along with Zoroastrianism—that subscribe to the belief that God will do the judging and accept the existence of a non-earth heaven and hell, do not believe in eternal punishment. They believe the majority of bad souls will be cleansed then sent to heaven. All remaining unredeemable bad souls will be extinguished. These outcomes are discussed above under Purified and Destroyed.

For consistency in the analysis, this third outcome is scored based on the soul's probability of getting to heaven—that is achieving a good afterlife.

As discussed earlier, the criteria or yardstick that God will use varies between the religions. In general, it will be a balancing or weighing of good deeds or righteous acts against bad/evil deeds or unrighteous acts. If your good deeds outweigh your bad deeds, you go to heaven. If your bad deeds outweigh your good deeds, you go to hell. Some religions advocate that in addition to your good and bad deeds, there are other factors that will be considered.

In Islam, your intentions will also be added to the scales.

Judaism teaches that Jewish people have a reserved place in heaven, but their reservation can be cancelled due to sins. Gentiles can receive salvation based on the fulfillment of seven commandments. Jewish teaching holds that

> only truly righteous souls ascend directly to the Garden of Eden [Heaven], say the sages. The average person descends to a place of punishment and/or purification, generally referred to as Gehinnom [Sheol, Hades, or Hell].

The soul's sentence in Gehinnom is usually limited to a 12-month period of purgation before it takes its place in Olam Ha-Ba [The World to Come] (Mishnah Eduyot 2:9, Shabbat 33a). This 12-month limit is reflected in the yearlong mourning cycle and the recitation of the Kaddish (the memorial prayer for the dead).

Only the utterly wicked do not ascend to the Garden of Eden at the end of this year. Sources differ on what happens to these souls at the end of their initial time of purgation. Some say that the wicked are utterly destroyed and cease to exist, [This eventuality is analogous to the third outcome of The Merry-Go-Round: Eraser possibility. A soul that is destroyed would have no way of experiencing, remembering, enjoying, or regretting anything, good or bad. In effect, it would be the same as if the soul was never created or the soul is mortal. In our analysis, it results in the equivalent of a good afterlife.] while others believe in eternal damnation. (Maimonides, Mishneh, Law of Repentance, 3:5–6)[7]

As previously noted, every religion encourages its followers to do good works. They also guide adherents down a path of knowledge and wisdom. That path leads to a higher level of understanding oneself, the world in which we live, and the greater universe. If we follow our chosen religion's directive, we should have the scales tip to the side of goodness when judged by every religion's criteria. Aware of the actions each religion considers bad/evil (see appendix C), we would avoid these acts—irrespective of which specific religion we follow.

Therefore, all humans who acknowledge a judging God would have an equal opportunity to go to heaven. However, tipping the scales in the good direction is not guaranteed. It is as likely that a person will have more bad deeds as it is the person will have more good deeds. This would consider any unique or additional requirements imposed by a specific religion. As a result, followers of every God-fearing religion are assigned a probably of 0.50 or 50 percent of experiencing a good afterlife.

With that said, we need to consider if there are specific bad/evil acts that are unforgiveable. These would be acts so egregious they outweigh all the individual's good deeds, words, thoughts, and intentions. You could not overcome these acts with prayers. Being compliant with the applicable six hundred and thirteen commandments wouldn't matter. Repenting for these bad/evil acts could not erase them. And fulfillment of the seven Judaism commandments would have no effect. Of the religions (Islam, African

---

7. Rose, "Heaven and Hell," §Gehinnom: A Jewish Hell.

Traditional & Diasporic, and Judaism) that promote the belief of an eternal punishment, Islam is the one religion that identifies such an evil act.

Shirk is the sin of idolatry or polytheism. It assigns or establishes partners with God (known to Muslims as Allah) or ascribes divine attributes for worship to others besides Allah. The other religions also prohibit idol worship or worshiping anything other than God. However, while they issue stern warnings against this act, they do not elevate it to the level of an unforgivable sin. According to Islam, individuals who commit this sin believe that their source of power, harm, and blessings comes from others besides Allah, the one singular God, who has no children or wives. The Qur'an states:

> Verily, Allah forgives not that partners should be ascribed to Him in worship, but He forgives except that (anything else) to whom He pleases; and whoever ascribes partners to Allah in worship, has indeed invented a tremendous sin. (V. 4:48).

Of the religions that believe in God, Christianity (including individuals identified with other religions who have accepted Christian beliefs), Hinduism, Chinese Folk-Religionist, some African Traditional & Diasporic, and Cao Dai are guilty of committing Shirk. Followers of these religions would have no chance of attaining a good afterlife. They have been assigned a probability of 0.00 or 0 percent for the Islam afterlife scenario.

The Lion and the Lamb

The last Judgment Day possibility we analyze requires a belief in both God and Jesus Christ. Here the judgment will be carried out by Jesus Christ or by God through Jesus Christ. In this afterlife reality, only Christians would meet the requirements to receive a good afterlife. Again, this includes individuals of other faiths who have accepted Christian beliefs, but identify with another faith; so, they are effectively Christians. They have been assigned a probability of 1.00 or 100 percent. Followers of all other religions or nonreligions have been assigned a probability of 0.00 or 0 percent.

Decision Day

We next look at the Decision Day afterlife possibility. In this afterlife reality, every soul gets to decide where or how it spends eternity. This scenario would naturally guarantee a good afterlife for every soul, since we desire a pleasant existence instead of a tormented one. However, if a soul did truly desire a tormented eternity, then it could not be considered bad (recall our definition in chapter 5) since it was the soul's choice. As a result, everyone is given a probability of 1.00 or 100 percent of having a good afterlife.

Extreme Measures

The final afterlife possibility to analyze is Extreme Measures. It has two alternatives. For each alternative, there is only one destination where all souls will spend eternity.

I. Good Place

In the first alternative, there is only a good place or good state. Give it a name that floats your boat: Heaven, Paradise, Gan Eden, Shangri-La, Atlantis, Nirvana, the Supreme Abode, or the Fifth Dimension. If this is the afterlife reality that awaits us, then everyone is guaranteed to win—that is have a good afterlife. Followers of every religion or nonreligion are assigned a probability of 1.00 or 100 percent.

II. Bad Place

In the second alternative there is only a bad place or bad state. Again, you pick the name. If this is the afterlife reality that awaits us, then everyone is guaranteed to lose—that is have a bad afterlife. Everyone receives a probability of 0.00 or 0 percent.

And the Winner Is[8]

If the human soul is not immortal or a human being does not have a soul, then there is no afterlife (N/A). Nevertheless, since no afterlife is not the same as a bad afterlife, these conditions result in a good afterlife with followers of all religions and nonreligions being assigned a probability of 1.00 or 100 percent. While not included in the table below, they are included in the calculation to determine the probability of a good afterlife for each religion.

8. Note: In the following analysis, the word religion includes those ideologies which may be referred to as a nonreligion.

Place Your Bet

Afterlife Possibility	Religion	Probability of a Good Afterlife
Without a Trace	Every religion	100%
Déjà Vu	Every religion	50%
The Merry-Go-Round: Ain't No Stopping Us Now	Every religion	100%
The Merry-Go-Round: Reunited, and It Feels So Good	Every religion	100%
The Merry-Go-Round: Eraser	Every religion	100%
Judgment Day: Control	Every religion	50%
Judgment Day: The Scales of Justice: Purified	God-fearing religion	100%
Judgment Day: The Scales of Justice: Purified	Non-God-fearing religion	0%
Judgment Day: The Scales of Justice: Destroyed	God-fearing religion	100%
Judgment Day: The Scales of Justice: Destroyed	Non-God-fearing religion	0%
Judgment Day: The Scales of Justice: Punished: Islam	God-fearing religions except Christianity, Hinduism, Chinese Folk-Religionist, some African Traditional & Diasporic, Cao Dai	50%

Afterlife Possibility	Religion	Probability of a Good Afterlife
Judgment Day: The Scales of Justice: Punished: Islam	Non-God-fearing religions, Christianity, Hinduism, Chinese Folk-Religionist, some African Traditional & Diasporic, Cao Dai	0%
Judgment Day: The Scales of Justice: Punished: African Traditional & Diasporic	God-fearing religion	50%
Judgment Day: The Scales of Justice: Punished: African Traditional & Diasporic	Non-God-fearing religion	0%
Judgment Day: The Scales of Justice: Punished: Judaism	God-fearing religion	50%
Judgment Day: The Scales of Justice: Punished: Judaism	Non-God-fearing religion	0%
The Lion and the Lamb	Christianity	100%
The Lion and the Lamb	Every religion except Christianity	0%
Decision Day	Every religion	100%
Extreme Measures: Good Place	Every religion	100%
Extreme Measures: Bad Place	Every religion	0%

By averaging the probabilities assigned to each religion, we find that Christianity offers its followers the best chance of achieving a good afterlife. With a 76.47 percent probability (see appendix E), it is 44 percent greater than religions that do not acknowledge the existence of a God who passes judgment on human souls. In determining whether a religion acknowledges this type of God, I've used a broad definition of the word judgment. If the religion indicates that God will participate in affecting the soul's ultimate destination, it has been included.

This is not to say that Christianity is "right," and all other religions are "wrong." As demonstrated earlier, no one knows what will happen to you after you die. Therefore, the question of which religion is "right" cannot be determined and furthermore is irrelevant—at this stage of the analysis where we are answering question number 2: What do I bet on? Christianity is simply the best bet. It offers the highest payoff with the least amount of risk in relation to all other alternatives.

Let's bring this down to the individual's level. We compare the fate of individuals from other faiths with that of a Christian. This is assessed in the context of a bet and the probability of winning. We win by receiving a good afterlife. We lose by receiving a bad afterlife. For our analysis, if there is no afterlife, then we count that as a win. Let's look at three examples. We begin with an Atheist.

Atheism teaches that there is no God and no afterlife—captured in the Without a Trace afterlife possibility. Christianity advocates there is a God with his son, Jesus Christ, and an afterlife. In the Christian afterlife Jesus Christ—or God through Jesus Christ—will judge all human souls. This perspective is captured in the Judgment Day: The Lion and the Lamb afterlife possibility.

The element of chance (the risk) within the gamble is represented by a two-sided coin. Heads represents Atheism's perspective of the afterlife. Tails represents Christianity's perspective of the afterlife.

For an Atheist, if the coin lands on heads, he wins. If the coin lands on tails, he loses. This equates to a winning probability of 50 percent. For a Christian, if the coin lands on heads, he wins. If the coin lands on tails, he wins. This equates to a winning probability of 100 percent.

We next consider the fate of a Buddhist with that of a Christian. Buddhism teaches that the soul—with the closest equivalent in Buddhism being consciousness—cycles through birth, death, and rebirth indefinitely until it reaches nirvana. Nirvana is a transcendent state of perfect peace and happiness. It's the equivalent of salvation for the soul referred to in other religions. This is the fate of all souls—captured in the Merry-Go-Round: Reunited, And It Feels So Good afterlife possibility.

Again, the risk within the gamble is represented by a two-sided coin. Heads represents Buddhism's perspective of the afterlife. Tails represents Christianity's perspective of the afterlife.

For a Buddhist, if the coin lands on heads, she wins. If the coin lands on tails, she loses. This equates to a winning probability of 50 percent. For a

Christian, if the coin lands on heads, she wins. If the coin lands on tails, she wins. This equates to a winning probability of 100 percent.

We conclude by considering the fate of a Bahá'í with that of a Christian. The Bahá'í religion teaches that a person will be judged by their own thoughts, words, and deeds. After death, the soul enters the spirit world and begins its progression toward God. Achieving a closeness to God is considered heaven. Being apart from God is hell. It is just as likely that a soul will attain this closeness as it is the soul will not. This perspective is captured in the Judgment Day: Control afterlife possibility.

The risk within this gamble is represented by two, two-sided coins.

- Coin #1
    - Heads = Bahá'í perspective
    - Tails = Christian perspective
- Coin #2
    - Heads = Close to God (Heaven)
    - Tails = Apart from God (Hell)

The gamble starts by tossing coin #1. For a Bahá'í, if the coin lands on heads, he then tosses coin #2. If coin #2 lands on heads, he wins. If it lands on tails, he loses. In the first toss, if coin #1 lands on tails, he losses without an opportunity to toss coin #2. This equates to a winning probability of 25 percent.

For a Christian, if coin #1 lands on heads, he then tosses coin #2. If coin #2 lands on heads, he wins. If it lands on tails, he loses. In the first toss, if coin #1 lands on tails, he wins with no need to toss coin #2. This equates to a winning probability of 50 percent.

This head-to-head comparison between religions serves as reinforcement to the logic underpinning the analysis in appendix E. Each of the twenty-two religions is contrasted with the other twenty-one religions—in relation to the afterlife possibilities identified in chapter 5.

The nineteenth-century English author Samuel Butler said it best, "What is faith but a kind of betting or speculation after all? It should be, I bet that my Redeemer liveth."

Reflections

When was the last time you placed a bet or made an important decision with limited information?

What do you most treasure in the world?

How do you define winning in life?

7

Imagination

The power of imagination makes us infinite.

—JOHN MUIR

Imagination is the beginning of creation. You imagine what you desire,
you will what you imagine and at last you create what you will.

—GEORGE BERNARD SHAW

True change takes place in the imagination.

—UNKNOWN

In chapter 4, I asked you to accept two fundamental truths as we sought
to answer The Question. First, everyone is going to die, that is, cease to exist
in their current physical form. Second, no one knows what will happen to
them after they die.

I now present two vital underlying conditions regarding the hereafter.
These conditions would need to exist to make what we choose to do, or not
do, with our lives even matter. First, the soul must be immortal. It could
not be destroyed by anyone or anything, including ourselves. Second, there
would need to be an eternal punishment or undesirable condition for a bad
soul. For our purpose, a bad soul is one that did not behave in accordance
with the desires of the entity—call it God, a supreme being, the eternal

spirit, a pure energy, the force, or something else—that holds our universe together and gives it life. I have touched on the first condition earlier and will now expand upon it.

For the first condition, we must examine the soul's existence not through human eyes, but through the lens of eternity. Eternity is a state without end where time has no relevance. As a human being subjected to the laws—and corresponding effects (e.g., aging)—of this physical world, it is nearly impossible to grasp the concept of eternity. However, for the soul, eternity is precisely what it understands. And it operates in a manner that seeks self-preservation and a desirable environment or experience.

If the soul was not immortal, then at some point it would simply disappear; and the soul would understand the implications of such an outcome. Knowing its ultimate demise, the soul would wrestle with questions like, "Why should I invest my time and energy in activities that build my character? What is the purpose or benefit of acquiring knowledge? What is the value of accumulating wealth, attaining a certain status, or solving the world's most impactful problems? And why should I care about leaving a legacy?"

Once the soul vanished, it would have no memory or association of any kind with its former existence. It would be as if the soul never existed. Any experiences, "good" or "bad"—and these terms would probably need to be redefined—it had during its existence would be meaningless. The ecstatic joy or excruciating pain it may have felt would be gone without any lasting effect. It would not matter what the soul—as part of a physical or nonphysical body—believed, did, or intended to do while it existed. The form—a human being, an animal, a plant, a spirit, or an energy/force—to which the soul was attached would be of no significance. The soul could have resided on Earth, Jupiter, the Sun, or some other celestial body. It could have existed within a spiritual realm over many thousands or millions of years.

In the end, it would all go away, as if the soul was never created. Nothing associated with its time in existence would matter. If in the end the soul ceased to exist, there would be no reason to do anything. The soul's activities—whether they brought feelings of pain or pleasure, sorrow or happiness, depression or excitement, failure or success—would not be supporting an entity that was built to last. And the soul, knowing this, would see no purpose in taking any action.

The second condition, which advocates an eternal punishment or undesirable situation for a bad soul, would need to exist for there to be meaningful consequences for the soul's behavior. Otherwise, it would not matter what the soul believed, did, or intended to do. If the punishment or undesirable condition was not for all eternity, a bad soul would eventually enjoy whatever conditions a good soul had. As it relates to the afterlife, there would be no incentive for any soul to be good. That would violate the universal laws of cause and effect (karma), action and reaction, yin and yang, and what goes around comes around. For a soul to pay any attention to how it will spend eternity, there would need to be an eternal undesirable condition—from which there is no possibility of escape.

Now separate from any motivations stemming from one's concern regarding their fate in the afterlife, a person may be incentivized to do good for various reasons. Those actions could offer the individual immediate or longer-term benefits. For example, you may provide a meal, clothing, or shelter to a homeless person. You do it because it makes you feel good about yourself and gives you a sensation of joy. This would be an immediate benefit to yourself and hopefully to the homeless individual. It would fulfill a real, tangible need for that person. Or you may volunteer with an organization like Habitat for Humanity and spend months constructing a house for a family in need. Watching the reactions of the family on move-in date could give you a tremendous sense of pride, happiness, and accomplishment. It could also provide a lasting, long-term benefit to your character—not to mention the benefit to the family.

Followers of those religions or nonreligions that do not factor these two underlying conditions into their perspective of the hereafter, have a significantly lower probability of attaining a good afterlife than followers of religions or nonreligions that do.

Imagine the following scenarios:

> Richard is a kind, thoughtful, and loving individual, who has dedicated his life to doing good deeds—to the best of his abilities. He does not believe God exists nor is there any form of an afterlife. Jennifer is also a kind, thoughtful, and loving individual, who has dedicated her life to doing good deeds—to the best of her abilities. She believes that God is real, does exists, and will pass judgment on her. Upon death, Richard and Jennifer proceed into the hereafter with two possibilities.
>
> In the first afterlife reality, there is no God. Consequently, there is no judgment by God, no conversation with God, and no interaction of any kind with God since there is no such being. Now this is what Richard had believed while he was alive; and it turns

out he was correct. Jennifer had believed in God but turns out she was wrong. But since there is no God, then there is no punishment or consequences of being wrong. Both Richard and Jennifer have an abundance of good deeds; so, whatever awaits them—if anything—in this afterlife, they will have an equal probability of experiencing it either good or bad.

In the second afterlife reality God does exists and will pass judgment on the deeds of all human souls. However, to be eligible for receiving judgment, the person—while they were alive—had to first believe that God does exist, and second believe that God will exercise judgment on human souls upon death. As Richard stands before God, he prepares to comment on his abundance of good deeds during his lifetime. However, before the proceedings begin, God, already knowing that Richard did not believe in its existence, presses a button and Richard falls through a trap door that leads straight to hell, where he will spend eternity being tormented. His life of good deeds could not save him, since he chose not to believe in a judging God while alive.

Next Jennifer comes before God. Having believed in a judging God while she was alive, Jennifer is judged by God. While she had many good deeds, God found that she did not have enough to warrant entry into heaven. Jennifer is also sent to hell. Her sentence in hell, however, is not permanent. After a set amount of time to atone for her sinful deeds, Jennifer is rewarded with heaven for the remainder of eternity.

Individuals who choose not to believe in a judging God have just under a 53 percent probability of achieving a good afterlife—if there is such a thing. Individuals who do believe in a God who passes judgment on human souls have on average just over a 73 percent probability. We can assess the situation with an afterlife Wheel of Fortune. The Wheel has seventeen distinct possibilities. These possibilities or scenarios were described in chapter 5. They were then scored in chapter 6 and tabulated in appendix E for each religion and nonreligion. Which wheel would you prefer to spin?

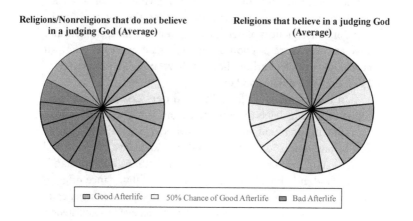

Let's get back to the example where you are the pilot and already in flight somewhere over the forty-eight contiguous United States. Before taking off, you were not afforded the opportunity to do any preflight planning. Also, your ultimate destination was not provided. The airplane is cruising toward the first known destination or waypoint: physical death. You have selected the airplane yourself, or one has been assigned to you. In this example, the airplane is the religion or nonreligion you have "chosen" to follow. If you are like most of us, this was not so much of a deliberate, thoughtful choice. But rather simply the ideology into which you were born. It's what the people—parents, grandparents, uncles, aunts, siblings, etc.—who helped raise you believed. Either way, it's the airplane you have today.

You are heading to one of seventeen cities represented by the seventeen afterlife possibilities discussed in chapter 5. Six of the destination cities are beyond the borders of the forty-eight contiguous United States. These six cities are represented by the Judgment Day afterlife possibilities that subscribe to the belief that God or Jesus Christ will pass judgment on all human souls. The other eleven cities, representing the other eleven afterlife possibilities, are located within the boundary of the forty-eight states. These cities can be considered a waypoint, which also aligns with the first known destination: physical death. The six Judgment Day cities can be thought of as points beyond or after physical death.

There are two kinds of airplanes: type I and type II. Both airplane types can reach the eleven cities within the borders of the forty-eight contiguous United States. However, only a type II plane can reach cities beyond the borders of the forty-eight contiguous United States. Your destination city will be revealed when you arrive at the waypoint—physical death. Once you arrive at this location, you will not be able to change the type of plane you are flying. Up to this waypoint, if you are currently in a type I plane, you can acquire a type II plane, which can reach sixteen cities. No airplane can reach all seventeen cities. What type of airplane do you want?

Whether or not this type of God truly exists will continue to be debated long after you and I are dead. And while we're on the topic, does God—in any form—really exist? Can religion prove definitively there is a God? And on the flip side, can science prove definitively there is no God? I certainly have my opinion, but I'll leave those questions for you to answer. We often get hung up on thinking that for us to believe something, we must be able to prove it. That is not the case.

To help doubters or nonbelievers with this dilemma in the seventeenth century, French philosopher, mathematician, and physicist Blaise Pascal had the following advice.

> But at least learn your inability to believe, since reason brings you to this, and yet you cannot believe. Endeavour then to convince yourself, not by increase of proofs of God, but by the abatement of your passions. You would like to attain faith, and do not know the way; you would like to cure yourself of unbelief and ask the remedy for it. Learn of those who have been bound like you, and who now stake all their possessions. These are people who know the way which you would follow, and who are cured of an ill of which you would be cured. Follow the way by which they began; by acting as if they believed, taking the holy water, having masses said, etc. Even this will naturally make you believe, and deaden your acuteness.[1]

In addition to Pascal's "fake it til you make it" remedy, as human beings, we have been gifted with the ability to imagine. Our imagination allows us to form an opinion, hold a belief, and develop a steadfast conviction about something even if we are not able to prove it as being the truth. When deciding whether to believe in the existence of a God who will judge us, I encourage you—like many world-class athletes who frequently rely on visualization to help them win major sports competitions—to use this most incredible and powerful ability. The odds are too low, the stakes are too high, and the consequences are too severe if you are wrong.

---

1. *Wikipedia*, s.v. "Pascal's Wager."

Reflections

What is the wildest thing you have ever imagined?

How do you envision eternity?

Should you reap what you sow? If yes, why? If no, why not?

Epilogue

Learn from yesterday, live for today, hope for tomorrow. The important thing is not to stop questioning.

—ALBERT EINSTEIN

When it is obvious that the goals cannot be reached, don't adjust the goals, adjust the action steps.

—CONFUCIUS

Carpe diem.

—HORACE

USING YOUR UNIQUELY ENDOWED human capability of imagination, envision a similar situation described in chapter 7. In place of Richard and Jennifer, insert yourself. In this situation, Jesus Christ is involved in the judgment of the soul instead of God alone. In my mind's eye, I can see three possible scenes.

First, only Jesus Christ greets you to pass judgment. Second, Jesus Christ and God greet you. Third, only God greets you.

Let's play out each scene with two scenarios. In both scenarios you have tried to follow the direction of the religious or nonreligious leaders within your faith and accumulate more good deeds than bad deeds. You have also endeavored to satisfy any other specific requirements identified by the religion or nonreligion. In the first scenario, you are a Christian. In the second scenario you are a God-fearing person—you believe in a God who will pass judgment on all souls—but you are not a Christian.

Homecoming

Scene One (Christian)

You arrive at a set of ridiculously tall and breathtakingly beautiful gates—the pearly gates. They seem to extend upward forever, disappearing into what looks like a sea of glass. In your heart, you just know that what awaits on the other side of the gates is something spectacular. Your imagination is running wild, and you can barely contain your excitement. The anticipation is killing you.

Jesus Christ greets you with a smile that warms your heart. After welcoming you and exchanging pleasantries, he says, "Well done, my beloved child. Welcome home." He opens the gates and admits you into heaven for eternity. You run through the gates with boundless childlike energy, enthusiasm, and innocence.

Scene Two (Christian)

You arrive at a set of ridiculously tall and breathtakingly beautiful gates—the pearly gates. They seem to extend upward forever, disappearing into what looks like a sea of glass. In your heart, you just know that what awaits on the other side of the gates is something spectacular. Your imagination is running wild, and you can barely contain your excitement. The anticipation is killing you.

You are greeted by both Jesus Christ and God with smiles that warm your heart. After welcoming you, exchanging pleasantries, and confirming that you are indeed a Christian, Jesus acknowledges that you belong to him. He recommends to his Father, God, that you be admitted into heaven for all eternity. God will make the final decision, but your entrance into heaven is assured with Jesus' endorsement. God grants his son anything he requests. God says, "Well done, our beloved child. Welcome home." The gates are opened, and you are admitted into heaven for eternity. You run through the gates with boundless childlike energy, enthusiasm, and innocence.

Scene Three (Christian)

You arrive at a set of ridiculously tall and breathtakingly beautiful gates—the pearly gates. They seem to extend upward forever, disappearing into what looks like a sea of glass. In your heart, you just know that what awaits on the other side of the gates is something spectacular. Your imagination is running wild, and you can barely contain your excitement. The anticipation is killing you.

You are greeted by God alone with a comforting smile. He welcomes you and the two of you exchange pleasantries. However, you are a bit surprised and uneasy. You were expecting to see Jesus Christ, either alone or at least with God. Sensing that you are agitated, God asks, "Are you alright?" You hesitate, not sure how forceful to be since you are speaking to God. But you must ask the burning question on your mind. "Where is Jesus Christ?"

God responds in one of three ways:

1. "That deceiver is suffering in hell for pretending to be my Son and leading many souls astray. I am God alone. I have no son. No spouse. Nor anything else besides me. Anyone who believed in him, I have sent to hell along with him. I know you were a follower of his, so off to hell you go."

2. "That deceiver is suffering in hell for pretending to be my Son instead of my Messenger only. I am God alone. I have no son. No spouse. Nor anything else besides me. Now aside from this one deception, he otherwise spoke the truth and delivered my message to the world correctly. Let's look at how you lived your life to determine your fate."

3. "He is in heaven enjoying his reward for successfully delivering my message to the world. Why do you ask?" You feel strange for what you are about to say. Nevertheless, you continue. "Well, God, Jesus claimed to be your Son. He also said that he would be the one to judge human souls and the only way to you was through him." "Hmmm," says God. "Jesus. Come here. You got some explaining to do."

Left Behind

Scene One (Non-Christian)

You arrive at a set of ridiculously tall and breathtakingly beautiful gates. You suppose these are what Christians referred to as the pearly gates. They seem to extend upward forever, disappearing into what looks like a sea of glass. In your heart, you just know that what awaits on the other side of the gates is something spectacular. Your imagination is running wild. Although you had not believed in the Christian heaven and hell while alive, you can't wait to see what's in store for those allowed to enter. The anticipation is killing you.

You are greeted by Jesus Christ with the face of a poker player. After welcoming you, exchanging pleasantries, and confirming that you are not a Christian, he says, "It is with a heavy heart that I pass judgment on you. However, when I came down to earth, I made it clear that no one gets to my Father, who is in heaven, except through me. Since you chose not to believe in me, you will spend eternity in hell. I am very sorry. Goodbye." Your heart sinks. Everything you've ever heard, seen, or imagined about this place hits you like a tsunami. The feeling of excitement to experience what is on the other side of the pearly gates is replaced with a fear so great it's indescribable. You are sent to hell for eternity.

Scene Two (Non-Christian)

You arrive at a set of ridiculously tall and breathtakingly beautiful gates. You suppose these are what Christians referred to as the pearly gates. They seem to extend upward forever, disappearing into what looks like a sea of glass. In your heart, you just know that what awaits on the other side of the gates is something spectacular. Your imagination is running wild. Although you had not believed in the Christian heaven and hell while alive, you can't wait to see what's in store for those allowed to enter. The anticipation is killing you.

You are greeted by both Jesus Christ and God with the faces of poker players. After welcoming you, exchanging pleasantries, and confirming that you are not a Christian, Jesus states that you do not belong to him. He reminds you of his warning that if you disowned him before men on earth that he would disown you before his Father in heaven. He recommends to his Father, God, that you be sent to hell for all eternity. God will make the final decision, but your sentence to hell is assured with Jesus' denial of knowing you. God grants his son anything he requests. God and Jesus Christ say goodbye. Your heart sinks. Everything you've ever heard, seen, or imagined about this place hits you like a tsunami. The feeling of excitement to experience what is on the other side of the pearly gates is replaced with a fear so great it's indescribable. You are sent to hell for eternity.

Scene Three (Non-Christian)

You arrive at a set of ridiculously tall and breathtakingly beautiful gates. You suppose these are what Christians referred to as the pearly gates. They seem to extend upward forever, disappearing into what looks like a sea of glass. In your heart, you just know that what awaits on the other side of the gates is something spectacular. Your imagination is running wild. Although you had not believed in the Christian heaven and hell while alive, you can't wait to see what's in store for those allowed to enter. The anticipation is killing you.

You are greeted by God alone with a comforting smile. It doesn't surprise you, because you were not expecting to see Jesus Christ or anyone else with God. After welcoming you and exchanging pleasantries, God says, "Let's look at how you lived your life to determine your fate."

Who Dat?

For individuals who do believe in God, the probability of achieving a good afterlife range from 70.59 percent to 76.47 percent. A significant point of differentiation between Christianity and all other God-fearing religions is centered around the question Jesus posed to his disciples in Matthew 16:13 (New International Version). "Who do people say the Son of Man is?" As imagined in the three scenes above, how you respond to that question— while you are in the land of the living—will be pivotal in determining your fate in the next life.

According to Christians, Jesus Christ is the only begotten Son of God. Furthermore, he is one with God and therefore is God incarnate. Christianity is the only religion that takes this position.

Most of the other God-fearing religions advocate that Jesus was God's messenger. He was sent to earth along with other messengers at various times throughout human history. These messengers are considered prophets who have a direct line to God. They speak the truth revealing God's will to humanity. Individuals who present themselves as a prophet, and do not speak God's truth, are labeled false prophets. This is the argument by Judaism. That Jesus Christ was a false prophet. Let's examine these claims.

Christians assert that Jesus declared in his own words to be "The"— one and only—Son of God. He presented enough evidence through his life, death, resurrection, and other tangible actions to convince them he was telling the truth. Therefore, Christians accept this as a fact.

Other God-fearing religions who proclaim that Jesus was only a messenger, and not the Son of God, make the following argument. Their position is that Jesus never said in his own words that he was "The" Son of God. Christians have either misinterpreted his words or deliberately changed his words to support their position.

Judaism argues that Jesus did profess to be "The" Son of God—The Messiah—but was not telling the truth. Furthermore, he was not a messenger of God and was in fact a false prophet.

Each group has much "evidence" to support their claim. Which one is correct? Well, that's an open question. As with the case of knowing what will happen to you when you die, the truth is indeterminate. It cannot be proven one way or another. You will need to review the evidence, assess the probabilities, consider the consequences, weigh the odds, seek guidance from within yourself or from a higher power, and reach your own conclusion of what to believe.

I wish you clarity of thought as you go through the process. It is a formidable task, but one you cannot neglect. And only you can do it. I urge you to do it now. For no one is promised tomorrow.

It's your soul. Place your bet.

Epilogue

Reflections

Review your answers from the reflections at the end of each chapter. Would you change any responses?

Who in your life should read this book?

What are your next steps?

Appendix A[1]

Major Religions of the World

Ranked by Number of Adherents

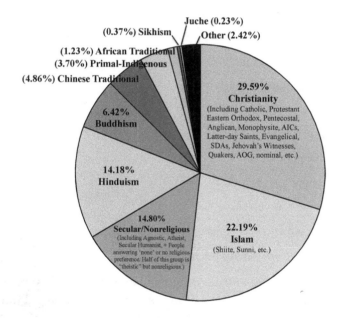

Juche (0.23%)
(0.37%) Sikhism
Other (2.42%)
(1.23%) African Traditional
(3.70%) Primal-Indigenous
(4.86%) Chinese Traditional

29.59%
Christianity
(Including Catholic, Protestant
Eastern Orthodox, Pentecostal,
Anglican, Monophysite, AICs,
Latter-day Saints, Evangelical,
SDAs, Jehovah's Witnesses,
Quakers, AOG, nominal, etc.)

6.42%
Buddhism

14.18%
Hinduism

14.80%
Secular/Nonreligious
(Including Agnostic, Atheist,
Secular Humanist, + People
answering 'none' or no religious
preference. Half of this group is
"theistic" but nonreligious.)

22.19%
Islam
(Shiite, Sunni, etc.)

(ALL MATERIAL FROM REFERENCED source except notes.) (*Sizes shown are approximate estimates and are here mainly for the purpose of ordering the groups, not providing a definitive number. This list is sociological/statistical in perspective.*)

1. "Adherents.com: Religion Statistics Geography, Church Statistics" (Library of Congress web archive), p. 1, https://www.loc.gov/item/lcwaN0003960/.

Appendix A

1. Christianity: 2.1 billion [2.4 billion]

2. Islam: 1.5 billion [1.8 billion]

3. Secular/Nonreligious/Agnostic/Atheist: 1.1 billion [1.2 billion]

4. Hinduism: 900 million [1.15 billion]

5. Chinese Traditional Religion: 394 million

6. Buddhism: 376 million [521 million]

7. Primal-Indigenous: 300 million

8. African Traditional & Diasporic: 100 million

9. Sikhism: 23 million [30 million]

10. Juche: 19 million

11. Spiritism: 15 million

12. Judaism: 14 million [14.4 million]

13. Baháʼí: 7 million

14. Jainism: 4.2 million

15. Shinto: 4 million

16. Cao Dai: 4 million

17. Zoroastrianism: 2.6 million

18. Tenrikyo: 2 million

19. Neo-Paganism: 1 million

20. Unitarian-Universalism: 800 thousand

21. Rastafarianism: 600 thousand

22. Scientology: 500 thousand

Note 1: Religions with a second number within brackets[2] reflect the most recent 2012 estimates from *Adherents.com*, which changed from the original published list downloaded on October 2, 2011.

Note 2: The world population was 7.128 billion as of December 2012 according to the United Nations as presented by *Worldometers*.[3] Using the number of adherents associated with each religion, Adherents.com report

2. *Wikipedia*, s.v. "Religious Populations."

3. *Worldometers*, s.v. "World Population," https://www.worldometers.info/world-population/world-population-by-year/.

a 2012 world population of 8.110 billion, due to rounding and using the upper bound estimates for each group. I have adjusted this figure down—in relative proportionate amounts per group—to align with the United Nations number (7.128 billion). These adjusted figures are used to estimate the percent of the population represented by the number of adherents in each afterlife possibility listed in chapter 5. For religions where multiple afterlife philosophies are taught, I have further segmented the total number of adherents. The segmentation and resulting percentages are a rough estimate and should be viewed as providing directional figures only.

Introduction

The adherent counts presented in the list above are current estimates of the number of people who have at least a minimal level of self-identification as adherents of the religion. Levels of participation vary within all groups. These numbers tend toward the high end of reasonable worldwide estimates. Valid arguments can be made for different figures, but if the same criteria are used for all groups, the relative order should be the same. Further details and sources are available below and in the Adherents.com main database.

A major source for these estimates is the detailed country-by-country analysis done by David B. Barrett's religious statistics organization, whose data are published in the *Encyclopedia Britannica* (including annual updates and yearbooks) and also in the *World Christian Encyclopedia* (the latest edition of which—published in 2001—has been consulted). Hundreds of additional sources providing more thorough and detailed research about individual religious groups have also been consulted.

This listing is not a comprehensive list of all religions, only the "major" ones (as defined below). There are distinct religions other than the ones listed above. But this list accounts for the religions of over 98% of the world's population. Below are listed some religions which are in this listing (Mandeans, PL Kyodan, Ch'ondogyo, Vodoun, New Age, Seicho-No-Ie, Falun Dafa/Falun Gong, Taoism, Roma), along with explanations for why they do not qualify as "major world religions" on this list. Hence, in this list, which is explicitly statistical and sociological in perspective, Taoism should be thought of as a major branch of Chinese traditional religion.

This world religions listing is derived from the statistics data in the Adherents.com database. The list was created by the same people who collected and organized this database, in consultation with university professors of comparative religions and scholars from different religions. We invite additional input. The Adherents.com collection of religious adherent statistics now has over 43,000 adherent statistic citations, for over 4,300 different faith groups, covering all countries of the world. This is not an absolutely exhaustive compilation of all such data, but it is by far the largest compilation available on the Internet. Various academic researchers and religious representatives regularly share documented adherent statistics with Adherents.com so that their information can be available in a centralized database.

Statistics and geography citations for religions not on this list, as well as subgroups within these religions (such as Catholics, Protestants, Karaites, Wiccans, Shiites, etc.) can be found in the main Adherents.com database.

Parameters of This List

In order to rank religions by size, two parameters must be defined:

1. What constitutes a "religion"?
2. How is "size" determined?

With a working definition of a "religion" and a method for measuring size, criteria for what constitutes a "major" religion must be determined, otherwise this list could be impractically inclusive and long.

"Major religions," for the purposes of this list, are:

- Large—at least 500,000 adherents
- Widespread—appreciable numbers of members live and worship in more than just one country or limited region
- Independent—the religion is clearly independent and distinct from a broader religion

Appendix B

Afterlife Beliefs

*of Major Religions of the World
as defined by Adherents.com*

1. Christianity

Christian beliefs about the afterlife vary between denominations and individual Christians, but the vast majority of Christians believe in some kind of heaven, in which the deceased enjoy the presence of God and loved ones for eternity. Views differ as to what is required to get to heaven, and conceptions of heaven differ as well.

A slightly smaller majority of Christians believe in hell, a place of suffering where unbelievers or sinners are punished. Views differ as to whether hell is eternal and whether its punishment is spiritual or physical. Some Christians reject the notion altogether.

Catholic Christians also believe in purgatory, a temporary place of punishment for Christians who have died with un-confessed sins.[1]

In his letter to the Romans, Paul wrote, "For the wages of sin is death, but the gift of God is eternal life in Christ Jesus our Lord." (Romans 6:23) This single sentence neatly summarizes the Christian doctrine of atonement, which teaches that the reconciliation of sinful humanity with the God of love was accomplished by God in the sacrifice of His son, Jesus Christ, on the cross.[2]

1. "Christianity on the Afterlife," https://religionfacts.com/christianity/afterlife.
2. *Patheos*, "Christianity," §Beliefs: Afterlife and Salvation.

Branches of Christianity differ on how humans can and are to respond to this gift of God, but all Christians agree that the resurrection of Jesus made eternal life possible for humans. Eternal life begins not after death, but at the moment of spiritual new birth, understood in some Christian traditions as occurring at the time of baptism and in others as occurring at a point of conscious trust in Christ, and death is but a passage of the eternal soul. Although the physical body dies, the soul of a person is rewarded or punished based on a life of faith. Those who believed in Jesus and his work and who expressed that faith in good works will be rewarded with heaven and will live in the presence of God; those who refused to believe in Jesus and lived wickedly will be punished in hell. Finally, Christianity also teaches that at the end of time, after divine judgment, those who have eternal life will also be physically resurrected, just as Jesus was.

Many contemporary Christians struggle with the thought that a loving God would not receive either all or the vast majority of people into heaven. They often decide to leave that question to the love and mercy of God. Jesus promised he would return to judge all people, and Christians see this not as a reason to fear, but as a promise of the return of a Savior, the friend and brother of sinners. Most importantly, Christian belief about salvation holds that eternal life cannot be earned by human striving, because no one would deserve salvation if judged entirely on merit. Eternal life is a gift from God.[3]

2. Islam

Muslims believe in a final judgment, referred to by many names in the Qur'an: the Day of Reckoning, the Day of Distress, the Day of the Gathering, the Great Announcement, and the Hour. Common with other theologies that subscribe to the idea of a judgment, they also believe in heaven and hell. Each person is responsible for the judgment he or she will receive. People are judged based on their intentions and their deeds.

> Islam does not teach that we are in need of intercession, although some traditions have allowed that Muhammad might intercede with God on our behalf. No one can know God, but at the same time, no one stands between the individual Muslim and God. If we find that we have sinned, we may sincerely apologize, and through

3. *Patheos*, "Christianity," §Beliefs: Afterlife and Salvation.

our remorse, receive forgiveness. The slate is clean, and we may begin again. This will likely happen to us many times in our lives, because we are not perfect. But on the Last Day, there are no excuses. God has sent many prophets to remind us of our duty and to wake us up when we forget our dependence on God. As a result, the punishment on the Last Day is just.[4]

Muslims believe in the Day of Judgment and heaven and hell. A person's ultimate destiny, whether it is heaven or hell, depends on the degree to which that person intended and acted as God desires, with justice and mercy toward others. While it is impossible to know with certainty who will go to heaven and hell, believers, who had faith in the revelations that God sent through his prophets [including Adam, Abraham, Moses, David, Jesus, and Muhammad] and lived according to those revelations, may hope for heaven. There is some evidence that nonbelievers can attain paradise, and even those who do evil but who are met at the end with God's grace and mercy may attain paradise.[5]

However, Islam teaches there is one great sin which will not be forgiven by God (known to Muslims as Allah). This unpardonable sin is Shirk. In Islam Shirk is the sin of idolatry or polytheism which assigns or establishes partners with Allah or ascribes divine attributes for worship to others besides Allah. Individuals who commit this sin also believe that their source of power, harm, and blessings comes from others besides Allah, the one singular God, who has no children or wives, according to Islam.

The Qur'an states:

> Verily, Allah forgives not that partners should be ascribed to Him in worship, but He forgives except that (anything else) to whom He pleases; and whoever ascribes partners to Allah in worship, has indeed invented a tremendous sin. (V. 4:48).

3. Secular/Nonreligious/Agnostic/Atheist

"This is a highly disparate group and not a single religion."[6] So, there is no consistent belief in an afterlife. In general people who fall within this group

4. *Patheos*, "Islam," §Beliefs: Afterlife and Salvation.

5. *Patheos*, "Islam," §Beliefs: Afterlife and Salvation.

6. "Adherents.com: Religion Statistics Geography, Church Statistics" (Library of Congress web archive), p. 1.

do not believe in God or an afterlife. To help describe this group's followers, below is a list of definitions for some of the various classifications.

"Agnostic" in normal usage today means "don't know" or having an open mind about religious belief, especially the existence of God. It can also mean something much firmer: that nothing is known, or can possibly be known, about God or supernatural phenomena, and that it is wrong of people to claim otherwise. That is the original meaning of the word, and 19th century "agnostics" lived their lives atheistically in practice—that is, without any reference to any concepts of gods.

"Atheist" includes those who reject a belief in the existence of God or gods and those who simply choose to live without God or gods. Along with this often, but not always, go disbelief in the soul, an afterlife, and other beliefs arising from god-based religions.

"Freethinker" is an old-fashioned term, popular in the nineteenth century, used of those who reject authority in matters of belief, especially political and religious beliefs. It was a very popular term in the 19th century and is still used in different languages in some European countries by non-religious organisations to describe themselves.

"Humanist" is used today to mean those who seek to live good lives without religious or superstitious beliefs. A humanist may embrace all or most of the other approaches introduced here, and in addition humanists believe that moral values follow on from human nature and experience in some way. Humanists base their moral principles on reason (which leads them to reject the idea of any supernatural agency), on shared human values and respect for others. They believe that people should work together to improve the quality of life for all and make it more equitable. Humanism is a full philosophy, "life stance" or worldview, rather than being about one aspect of religion, knowledge, or politics.

"Non-religious"—as well as those who are uninterested in religion or who reject it, this category may include the vague or unaffiliated, those who are only nominally or culturally affiliated to a religious tradition, and the superstitious.

"Rationalist" in this context, describing a non-religious belief, means someone who prioritises the use of reason and considers reason crucial in investigating and understanding the world. Rationalists usually reject religion on the grounds that it is unreasonable. (Rationalism is in contradistinction to fideism—positions which rely on or advocate "faith" in some degree).

"Skeptic" today usually means someone who doubts the truth of religious and other supernatural or "paranormal" beliefs, typically on rationalist grounds. ("Skeptic" also has a special philosophical meaning: someone who rejects or is skeptical with regard to all claims to knowledge).

"Secularists" believe that laws and public institutions (for example, the education system) should be neutral as between alternative religions and beliefs. Almost all humanists are secularists, but religious believers may also take a secularist position which calls for freedom of belief, including the right to change belief and not to believe. Secularists seek to ensure that persons and organisations are neither privileged nor disadvantaged by virtue of their religion or lack of it. They believe secular laws—those that apply to all citizens—should be the product of a democratic process, and should not be determined, or unduly influenced, by religious leaders or religious texts. The word "secularism" was once used to describe a non-religious worldview generally but this meaning is now very old fashioned.[7]

4. Hinduism

"While Hinduism has been called the oldest religion in the world, many practitioners refer to their religion as Sanātana Dharma ('the eternal way'), which refers to the idea that its origins lie beyond human history, as revealed in the Hindu texts."[8]

One of the fundamental principles of Hinduism is the concept of samsara, the cycle of birth, life, death, and rebirth. Humans are reborn over and over. They can, however, "escape" rebirth by ridding themselves of karma and attaining moksha—the end of delusion. In some Hindu schools of thought, attaining moksha will not only end samsara, but will also bring benefits to the individual in her current lifetime. The person will be able to live a more complete, satisfying, and rewarding life.

The *Bhagavad Gita* states:

> As a person puts on new clothes and discards old and torn clothes, similarly an embodied soul enters new material bodies, leaving the old bodies. (B.G. 2:22)

7. Humanist UK, "Non-religious Beliefs," https://humanism.org.uk/humanism/humanism-today/non-religious-beliefs/.

8. *Wikipedia*, s.v. "Hinduism."

Appendix B

In the earliest strata of Hinduism, the Vedas [the most ancient of the world's Scriptures],[9] there is very little discussion of the afterlife, and really only a vague notion of salvation. Some texts, such as the Rig Veda, suggest that different people go to different places after they die, but there is little detail regarding the matter. This was simply not the focus of the religion. Rather, the concern was the proper performance of rituals that would keep the gods satisfied, and thus keep the cosmos in order.[10]

Some in the Vedic world eventually rejected this sacrificial emphasis and set out to find a new path, a path that would lead to eternal salvation. This path is among the focus of the Upanishads. In these texts, there is much discussion of what happens after death. In a famous passage from the Katha Upanishad, a sage named Nachiketas wins a boon from the god of death, Yama, and asks the god what happens to humans after they die. Yama at first refuses to answer, and then, after Nachiketas persists, tells the sage that if he wishes to know the answer to this question, he must study the nature of the self, and in the process, he will be able to leave both joy and sorrow behind.

This is a typically cryptic message from the Upanishads, but it points to a basic understanding of salvation articulated there: human beings continue to be reborn because they continue to generate karma, and they continue to generate karma because they are ignorant. They are ignorant of the true nature of the self. According to the Upanishads, the individual self, or atman, is no different than the ultimate reality of Brahman.

However, human beings are deluded, and think they are different. They think "I am," and thus they grasp on to the things of the material world. "I want . . . that is mine," and so on. But there is nothing that is not encompassed by the ultimate, by Brahman. According to the Upanishads, if one knows the true nature of the self—that it does not, in any ultimate sense, exist—then one will stop grasping. If one stops grasping, then one stops generating karma. And when there is no karma, there is no rebirth. One is released.

This release, called moksha, is ultimate salvation. The individual is absorbed in the ultimate, Brahman, in the same manner that a stream or a river (a metaphor for the individual atman) is absorbed into the ocean (Brahman). When one attains this state,

9. *Wikipedia*, s.v. "Hinduism," 2.2. Views, §Sanātana Dharma.
10. *Patheos*, "Hinduism," §Beliefs: Afterlife and Salvation.

rebirth stops. One is released, forever. The individual is one with Brahman.

This path, the Jnana marga or path of knowledge, is not the only means to attain ultimate salvation. Indeed, Hinduism very much holds that there are many paths to reach the same destination.

Paths (Margas)

Karma marga	Path of action (especially ritual action)	Vedas
Jnana marga	Path of knowledge (meditation and analysis)	Upanishads
Bhakti marga	Path of devotion (especially towards Krishna)	Bhagavad Gita

The Bhagavad Gita introduces the path of devotion, or bhakti marga. One can attain salvation, in the context of this path, through selfless loving devotion to a chosen god. In the Bhagavad Gita this god is Krishna, although because all of the gods in Hinduism are ultimately encompassed by the overarching divine powerhouse Brahman, bhakti directed at any god can lead to salvation.[11]

Bhakti is often discussed in distinctly human terms, using human love as the model. A parent's love for a child, for instance, is the model for the devotee's love of the god; a parent's love is utterly selfless, absolute. Likewise, the love of a devotee for a god is also described in amorous terms.

Some of the best-known and most beloved stories in Hinduism involve the love "affair" between Krishna and Radha (a particularly beautiful example is the Gita Govinda, by the poet Jayadeva). Krishna in these stories is a lovely young man who plays a bewitching flute. Radha is a beautiful young woman. She is, however, a human being. She abandons her worldly duty to be with Krishna. The point of these stories is that although worldly duties are importance for the maintenance of society, love of the divine (here specifically Krishna) transcends the worldly dharma. Through such absolute love, one attains salvation through the grace of the god.[12]

---

11. *Patheos*, "Hinduism," §Beliefs: Afterlife and Salvation.
12. *Patheos*, "Hinduism," §Beliefs: Afterlife and Salvation.

Another way to salvation is along the path of action.

Of the paths to spiritual liberation in Hinduism, karma yoga is the path of unselfish action. It teaches that a spiritual seeker should act according to dharma, without being attached to the fruits or personal consequences. Karma Yoga, states the Bhagavad Gita, purifies the mind. It leads one to consider dharma of work, and the work according to one's dharma, doing god's work and in that sense becoming and being "like unto god Krishna" in every moment of one's life.

According to Lord Krishna in Bhagavad Gita, Karma yoga is the spiritual practice of "selfless action performed for the benefit of others." Karma yoga is a path to reach moksha (spiritual liberation) through work. It is rightful action without being attached to fruits or being manipulated by what the results might be, a dedication to one's duty, and trying one's best while being neutral to rewards or outcomes such as success or failure.[13]

5. Chinese Traditional
(Confucianism, Taoism & Chinese Folk-Religionist)

Confucianism

Confucius stated that the afterlife was beyond human comprehension. Humans should live and behave in such a way as to promote ideal social relations, rather than to act based on the expectations of rewards or punishments after death. In Confucian terms, a meaningful life is one in which one develops one's innate moral potential to the fullest while fulfilling all of one's social obligations. At the same time, from a Confucian perspective, one cannot live fully in the present without being fully responsible to the past, both in terms of paying respect to one's ancestors and making the best of what they have left behind. What happens to human beings after they die is less important to Confucian thinkers than how the living fulfill their obligations to the dead.[14]

In *Centrality and Commonality: An Essay on Confucian Religiousness* (SUNY Press, 1989), the contemporary "New Confucian" thinker Tu Weiming describes the religious dimension of

13. *Wikipedia*, s.v. "Karma Yoga."
14. *Patheos*, "Confucianism," §Beliefs: Afterlife and Salvation.

Confucianism: "Being religious, in the Confucian perspective . . .
means being engaged in the process of learning to be fully human.
We can define the Confucian way of being religious as ultimate
self-transformation as a communal act and as a faithful dialogi-
cal response to the transcendent." This lifetime process of ultimate
self-transformation requires both membership in community
(starting with a human family) and individual engagement with
the source of ultimate meaning, Tian. Although Mengzi's vision
of Confucianism largely established the parameters of Confucian spirituality for all subsequent generations, it was the work of
his interpreter Zhu Xi that articulated most influentially what it
means to live religiously as a Confucian.

Zhu saw the universe as constantly involved in a dynamic
creative process of interplay between li (cosmic principle, including principles of morality, social order, etc.) and qi (vital energy,
but also the material world in its tangible forms). For Zhu, the
human heart-mind is where li and qi meet, become one, and help
order the universe: "The heart-mind unites nature (i.e., qi) and
emotion (i.e., li)." From a Confucian perspective, one can play no
more important role than to co-create moral order in the cosmos.
The proper unity of human nature with moral sentiments leads,
through the discipline of Confucian self-cultivation, to the desired
goal of cheng (authenticity or sincerity) as manifested in he (harmony) and zhong (centeredness) revealed through an exemplary
moral life. In such a life, a Confucian sees both salvation here and
now (in the sense that one has attained the Confucian goal of actu-
alizing one's innate, Tian-given and Tian-identified, potential) and
eternal life hereafter (in the sense that one becomes an example
and model for others who seek to walk the Confucian path of
self-transformation).[15]

Taoism

Early Taoism focused on this-worldly goal of achieving immortality of the
physical body. Later, in reaction to Buddhism, Taoism incorporated concepts of heaven, hell, and rebirth.

In no area is the lack of a single unified Taoist belief system more
evident than in the case of concepts about the afterlife and salvation. Several factors have contributed to this: 1) Taoism was at no

15. *Patheos*, "Confucianism," §Beliefs: Afterlife and Salvation.

point the only religion of China, but, rather, coexisted with Confucianism and Buddhism, as well as with Chinese folk religion; 2) each Taoist sect had its own beliefs and textual traditions, and these underwent changes over time; and 3) death and the afterlife became the province of Buddhism early in Chinese history, so that most ideas about the afterlife are Buddhist, or were developed in reaction to Buddhism.

Art found by archaeologists excavating tombs of the nobility has been quite varied, and does not support any unified set of beliefs about the afterlife. Murals or carvings featuring the Seven Sages of the Bamboo Grove, immortals, and other legendary characters of popular Taoism have been found in tombs, but there are Confucian, Buddhist, and other mythical images present in the same tombs. In later dynasties, continuing into the present, it is not uncommon to invite both Buddhist and Taoist priests to officiate at a funeral, and the structure of contemporary Taoist funerals is similar in many ways to those of Buddhism.

It is not surprising that once Buddhism had become established in China, many of its ideas about the afterlife were adopted by Taoism, because there were so many well-developed Buddhist ideas on the topic. Lingbao Taoism in particular incorporated many Buddhist ideas about the afterlife, and Lingbao priests perform rituals pertaining to the afterlife that priests of other sects do not, such as rituals transferring merit to the deceased. Shangqing Taoist scriptures include elaborate descriptions of the heavens and, to a lesser extent, the underworld; the use of Buddhist or Sanskrit terminology in naming some of these is a clear sign of their Buddhist origin. The concept of rebirth also became a factor in later Taoism.

Taoist notions of life beyond death are thus most easily discerned by looking at the time prior to the establishment of Buddhism in China. Generally speaking, early Taoist concepts of salvation focused on this life rather than an afterlife. Early Taoist groups were founded on utopian ideas of a new and perfect society, echoing sentiments found in the *Taode jing*. The focus for some individual practitioners, both *fangshi*, Taoshi, and some members of the nobility, was immortality of the physical body. They were not interested in what happens after death because they hoped never to die. Instead, they hoped to live forever in human form, with the supernatural powers of an immortal. Related to the quest for immortality was a popular interest in realms of the immortals that were believed to be located on earth—on mountains, islands, or other locations that are usually invisible to the human eye.

Afterlife Beliefs

Some Taoist gods are believed to reside on the sun, moon, planets, and constellations, and the Taoist adept is able to travel to these places during ritual trances. Some of the mystical excursions of Shangqing Taoism, for example, are to astronomical realms. The Big Dipper and its central star, the Pole Star, are especially important to Taoism. The deity Taiyi is believed to have a residence on the Pole Star, and the gods who reside within the body also reside in the (literal) heavens. The origin of these beliefs can be traced to a highly developed astronomical knowledge and religious engagement with astronomical realms that date back to the Shang dynasty (1700–1027 B.C.E.).

Salvation for Taoism (absent the Buddhist influence) is a matter of participation in the eternal return of the natural world, a yielding to chaos followed by spontaneous creation, in a never-ending cycle. This is not a permanent transcendent state or redemption such as has been articulated in the Abrahamic traditions. For Taoism, salvation is not an escape from this world; rather, it is to become perfectly aligned with the natural world and with the cosmic forces that sustain it.[16]

Chinese Folk-Religionist

The Chinese conception of the afterlife is based on a combination of Chinese folk religions, Taoism and Mahayana Buddhism.

At the moment of death, it is believed that one's spirit is taken by messengers to the god of walls and moats, Ch'eng Huang, who conducts a kind of preliminary hearing. Those found virtuous may go directly to one of the Buddhist paradises, to the dwelling place of the Taoist immortals, or the tenth court of hell for immediate rebirth.

After 49 days [most likely aligned with the amount of time found in the Buddhist's text, *The Tibetan Book of The Dead*], sinners descend to hell, located at the base of Mount Meru. There they undergo a fixed period of punishment in one or more levels of hell. The duration of this punishment may be reduced by the intercession of the merciful Ti-ts'ang. When the punishment is complete, the souls in hell drink an elixir of oblivion in preparation for their next reincarnation. They then climb on the wheel of transmigration, which takes them to their next reincarnation, or,

16. *Patheos*, "Taoism," §Beliefs: Afterlife and Salvation.

in an alternative account, they are thrown off the bridge of pain into a river that sweeps them off to their next life.[17]

Over the years, diverse Chinese myths and beliefs have gotten lumped into the nebulous category of "folk religion." This category includes everything from Traditional Chinese Medicine to beliefs about yin and yang. In pre-Buddhist Northern Chinese beliefs, everyone's soul had two parts, the *po* (the yin soul, made of earth) and the *hun* (the yang soul, made of *qi*.) Both souls needed sustenance to live and when the souls died, they went to different places, with the *hun* going to heaven in earliest ideas, and the *po* staying with the body or going to the underworld (although neither was specified as a place of reward or punishment.)

Heaven (天, tiān) is considered the source of all moral meaning and good, and it is the place where many gods reside (including the first god, the Jade Emperor.) Traditional Chinese religion honors many gods, and a few preside specifically over the dead, including the demigod Zhong Kui who subdues evil spirits and recruits them for a ghost army.[18]

6. Buddhism

There is no consistent notion of the afterlife or salvation in Buddhism. It varies according to country, era, and individual perspective.

Buddhism began as a way to address the suffering that exists in the world and was not overly-focused on ultimate salvation. That said, however, there was a clear doctrine of salvation in the Buddha's teachings: Salvation in early Buddhism was nirvana, the extinguishing of the all karma that constitutes the self. Nirvana is not a place or a state, but the end of rebirth.

Significantly, the Buddha said little about nirvana, because he felt that the alleviation of suffering was far more important, and that focusing on the goal of ultimate salvation would only lead to more attachments, and therefore more suffering. Rather than focus on nirvana as a goal, therefore, lay Buddhists were encouraged to give donations of goods, services, or money to monks or monasteries; to chant or copy sutras; and to engage in other activities

---

17. "Afterlife (Chinese Religion)," https://religionfacts.com/chinese-religion/afterlife.
18. Bullock, "Chinese Mythologies on Death."

in order to gain merit that could lead to a more desirable rebirth, which would bring them closer to enlightenment.

Some Mahayana Buddhist monks aspired to become bodhisattvas, postponing the dissolution of self until all living things are enlightened. For seminal religious figures and heads of religious orders in Tibet, this took the unusual form of continued incarnations in human form as the same individual, lifetime after lifetime. The current Dalai Lama is called the 14th, for example, because this is believed to be his 14th incarnation as the Dalai Lama.

The notion of skillful means in Mahayana Buddhism led to other interpretations of salvation, such as rebirth in a Pure Land, where one could continue to aspire to enlightenment in pleasant surroundings without fear of rebirth in human form. Mahayana texts also refer to hells into which one might be reborn, usually in the context of rescuing others from a hellish domain or transferring merit to those in such a place. There is also reference in the earliest texts to Yama, a deity of death who will judge and punish those who do evil. The punishment is not eternal but lasts until the karma of these misdeeds has been exhausted.

As Buddhism evolved and as it moved to other countries with different religious backgrounds, other views of the afterlife emerged. Yama became a central figure in popular understandings of the afterlife in East Asia and also in Tibet. Tibetan Buddhists also envisioned the Bardo, a kind of limbo where the soul or self remained until the next rebirth.

In the Chinese tradition, where ancient notions of the role of the ancestors in human life have shaped Buddhism, people burned incense and paper goods depicting goods or money for the benefit of their deceased loved ones in order to provide a better situation for them in the afterlife. The deceased, in turn, were believed to be able to bring benefits or cause harm to the living.

Notions of heavens and hells eventually became a part of popular Buddhism throughout Asia. These range from ideal surroundings such as the Pure Lands to horrific worlds of punishment and suffering. Illustrated "hell texts" are popular among some in Buddhist countries, depicting in detail the punishments one can expect for a host of specific misdeeds, which may range from wearing tight blue jeans to murder.

As should be evident, there is no single, consistent notion of the afterlife and salvation within Buddhism. There are diverse and contradictory ideas even within individual countries. This is the result of the merging of Buddhism with pre-existing conceptions, of contradictions between scholarly and popular understandings, and of the evolution of ideas within Buddhism throughout the life of the religion.[19]

While there are different and specific aspects of Buddhist beliefs from various regions, most Buddhist traditions share the goal of overcoming suffering and the cycle of death and rebirth, either by the attainment of Nirvana or through the path of Buddhahood. The path to reach this ultimate state can vary, with rebirth taking place in the physical world or in another more ideal, peaceful place (e.g., Pure Lands) with or without a temporary visit to a place of punishment to atone for the bad karma generated in one's most recent life/incarnation. The path most often taught is the Noble Eightfold Path.

The Noble Eightfold Path is grouped into three basic divisions as follows:[20]

Division	Eightfold Factor	Sanskrit, Pali	Description
Wisdom (Sanskrit: *prajñā*, Pāli: *paññā*)	1. Right view	*samyag dṛṣṭi, sammā ditthi*	The belief that there is an afterlife and not everything ends with death, that Buddha taught and followed a successful path to nirvana; according to Peter Harvey, the right view is held in Buddhism as a belief in the Buddhist principles of karma and rebirth, and the importance of the Four Noble Truths and the True Realities.
	2. Right intention	*samyag saṃkalpa, sammā saṅkappa*	Giving up home and adopting the life of a religious mendicant in order to follow the path; this concept, states Harvey, aims at peaceful renunciation, into an environment of non-sensuality, non-ill-will (to lovingkindness), away from cruelty (to compassion).

19. *Patheos,* "Buddhism," §Beliefs: Afterlife and Salvation.
20. *Wikipedia,* s.v. "Noble Eightfold Path."

Division	Eightfold Factor	*Sanskrit, Pali*	Description
	3. Right speech	*samyag vāc, sammā vāca*	No lying, no rude speech, no telling one person what another says about him, speaking that which leads to salvation.
Moral virtues (Sanskrit: *śīla,* Pāli: *sīla*)	4. Right action	*samyag kar-man, sammā kammanta*	No killing or injuring, no taking what is not given; no sexual acts in monastic pursuit, for lay Buddhists no sensual misconduct such as sexual involvement with someone married, or with an unmarried woman protected by her parents or relatives.
	5. Right livelihood	*samyag ā jīvana, sammā ājīva*	For monks, beg to feed, only possessing what is essential to sustain life. For lay Buddhists, the canonical texts state right livelihood as abstaining from wrong livelihood, explained as not becoming a source or means of suffering to sentient beings by cheating them, or harming or killing them in any way.
	6. Right effort	*samyag vyāyāma, sammā vāyāma*	Guard against sensual thoughts; this concept, states Harvey, aims at preventing unwholesome states that disrupt meditation.
Meditation (Sanskrit and Pāli: *samādhi*)	7. Right mindfulness	*samyag smṛti, sammā sati*	Never be absent minded, conscious of what one is doing; this, states Harvey, encourages mindfulness about impermanence of the body, feelings and mind, as well as to experience the five skandhas, the five hindrances, the four True Realities and seven factors of awakening.
	8. Right concentration	*samyag samādhi, sammā samādhi*	Correct meditation or concentration (*dhyana*), explained as the four jhānas.

7. Primal-Indigenous/Ethnic
(Ethno-religionist, Animists, and Shamanists)

Ethno-religionist

Many distinct religions are included in the ethno-religionist category. And, as such, there are many different views of the afterlife.
These views cover a broad spectrum of beliefs from the concept
of nirvana, heaven (paradise) and hell, heaven only and no hell,
no heaven and no hell, to the belief that bad souls are lost, extinguished, destroyed or simply cease to exist. Some of the ethnic
groups included in this category include the Druze of the Levant,
the Copts of Egypt, the Yazidi of northern Iraq, the Alevis of Tur-
key and the Yarsan [also known as Ahl-e Haqq] found primarily
in western Iran and Iraq.[21]

The Druze

Reincarnation is a paramount principle in the Druze faith. Reincarnations occur instantly at one's death because there is an eternal
duality of the body and the soul and it is impossible for the soul
to exist without the body. A human soul will transfer only to a human body, in contrast to the Hindu and Buddhist belief systems,
according to which souls can transfer to any living creature. Furthermore, a male Druze can be reincarnated only as another male
Druze and a female Druze only as another female Druze. A Druze
cannot be reincarnated in the body of a non-Druze. Additionally,
souls cannot be divided and the number of souls existing in the
universe is finite. The cycle of rebirth is continuous and the only
way to escape is through successive reincarnations. When this occurs, the soul is united with the Cosmic Mind and achieves the
ultimate happiness.[22]

21. "Adherents.com: Religion Statistics Geography, Church Statistics" (Library of
Congress web archive), p. 1.
22. *Wikipedia*, s.v. "Druze," 5.3. Reincarnation.

The Copts

"The Copts are an ethnoreligious group indigenous to Northeast Africa who primarily inhabit the area of modern Egypt, where they are the largest Christian denomination in the country and in the Middle East."[23]

The Yazidi (also spelled Yezidi)

Yazidis believe that the world was created by God, who entrusted it to seven angels led by one known as the Peacock Angel, also called Melek Taus. Melek Taus is the primary figure in the Yazidi belief system, as he filled the earth with flora and fauna.

Their religion is monotheistic and non-dualistic, and they do not believe in the concept of Hell. For them, all people have good and evil inside of them, and choices are made free of external temptation. They believe in internal purification through metempsychosis, a term referring to the transmigration of souls, according to Encyclopedia Britannica. They believe that the seven angels are occasionally reincarnated in human form.

Yazidis believe that they are descended directly from Adam alone, while the rest of humanity comes from the lineage of both Adam and Eve.[24]

The Alevis

Despite different descriptions of God within the Alevi religion, there is no evidence found of God ruling based on fear. Accordingly, God will not judge people by their acts of worship. There is also no literal heaven or hell with material pleasures or punishments. "Alevis believe in the immortality of the soul. Alevis, who believe in a literal existence of supernatural beings, also believe in good and bad angels (melekler). Alevis, believe in Satan who is the one that encourages human's evil desires (nefs). Alevis, believe in an existence of spiritual creatures, such as the Jinns (Cinler) and the evil eye."[25]

23. *Wikipedia*, s.v. "Copts."
24. Hafiz, "Yazidi Beliefs and Cosmology."
25. *Wikipedia*, s.v. "Alevism."

Appendix B

The Yarsan (also known as Ahl-e Haqq)

There is no concept of heaven or hell in the Yarsan religion.

Everyone has the essence of god, or bounty of god; some have many and some like only to taste it.

Incarnation and evolution are two separate issues and most scholars, philosophers, and Yārsānis reject incarnation with respect to a certain quality followed by Incarnations. They believe in evolution, rather than incarnation. As scholars of Yārsāni have stated, each human being needs to pass 1000 worlds in order to reach the last 1001st, stage, i.e., eternal perfection. Accordingly, each creature, depending on its stance, moves from one body to another in order to complete perfection.

The concepts and beliefs of Yārsān presented here have concentrated on the soul showing its Divine Essence. Therefore, the following features can be reported in brief for Doon-ā Doon in the Yārsānism School: First, a soul, depending on its talents and gifts, moves from one body to another—that of a human being, an animal, or other. Second, a soul is expected to pass 1001 epochs in varying worlds to reach and achieve perfection; again, the quiddity and quality of this procedure depends on his/her deeds, behavior and talent. Third, the soul who reaches the 1001st body in fact reaches the Truth 'Haghighat' stage, or the 'great happiness' (also called *Zāte Heq* or God). This means that a soul is in the last epoch of a mundane life. Lastly, a soul will experience the resurrection. What differentiates these beliefs from Incarnations, is that incarnation is without definite time but according to Manichean, the target is followed by these Trans carnations' reach to Land of lighting. Most scholars who considered Doon-ā-Doon and incarnation in Manichean (Parthian zādmūrd) the same have neglected this considerable difference. It's worth noting that according to my interview with a Yārsāni member, I understand that Yārsānism upholds that all individuals have the essence of God, and in the end the soul reaches Sultan Sahak. Yet, another great difference between Manichaeism and Yārsān.[26]

---

26. Hosseini, "Life after Death Yārsān."

Animists

"The cornerstone of animistic thought is the affirmation of the existence of some kind of metaphysical entities (such as souls or spirits) that are seen as the life-source (or life-force) of human beings, animals, plants and even non-living objects and phenomena. For animistic cultures, the existence of these entities (with their respective operational and volitional qualities) provides explanations for the innumerable changes witnessed in both the natural world and the human world."[27]

> Most animistic belief systems hold that this spirit survives physical death. In some instances, the spirit is believed to pass into a more leisurely world of abundant game and ever-ripe crops, while in other systems, such as that of the Navajo religion, the spirit remains on earth as a ghost, often becoming malignant in the process. Still other systems combine these two beliefs, holding that the afterlife involves a journey to the spirit world upon which the soul must not become lost. This journey entails much wandering as a ghost. The correct performance of funerary rites, mourning rituals, and ancestor worship were often considered necessary for expediting the deceased soul's completion of this journey.[28]

Shamanists

"Shamanism is a system of religious practice. Historically, it is often associated with indigenous and tribal societies, and involves belief that shamans, with a connection to the otherworld, have the power to heal the sick, communicate with spirits, and escort souls of the dead to the afterlife. It is an ideology that used to be widely practiced in Europe, Asia, North and South America, and Africa. It centered on the belief in supernatural phenomenon such as the world of gods, demons, and ancestral spirits."[29]

> There are many variations of shamanism throughout the world, but several common beliefs are shared by all forms of shamanism. Common beliefs identified by Eliade (1972) are the following:
>
> • Spirits exist and they play important roles both in individual lives and in human society

27. *New World Encyclopedia*, s.v. "Animism," 2.1. Existence of Souls or Spirits.
28. *New World Encyclopedia*, s.v. "Animism," 2.4. Survival of Dead.
29. *Wikipedia*, s.v. "Shamanism," 2. History.

- The shaman can communicate with the spirit world
- Spirits can be benevolent or malevolent
- The shaman can treat sickness caused by malevolent spirits
- The shaman can employ trances inducing techniques to incite visionary ecstasy and go on vision quests
- The shaman's spirit can leave the body to enter the supernatural world to search for answers
- The shaman evokes animal images as spirit guides, omens, and message-bearers
- The shaman can perform other varied forms of divination, scry, throw bones or runes, and sometimes foretell of future events[30]

Although included in the list by Adherents.com and commonly identified as a "religion," "it is important to highlight that shamanism is not a religion, and neither does it demand that one believe in the shaman's worldview. Faith is a judicial demand introduced by Christianity, but in shamanism, spirits and gods exist with the knowledge that, for others, buildings, animals and people exist."[31]

8. African Traditional & Diasporic

Discussing African notions of afterlife necessitates several preliminary and pertinent observations.

First, Africa is characterized by a tremendous ethnic and cultural diversity. There are about three thousand African ethnic groups, each boasting a distinctive common history, culture, language, and recognizable belief system. Thus, it is possible to speak of the Yoruba notions of afterlife and compare these, say, to the Igbo or Zulu concepts, noting distinctions and similarities.

Across the many ethnic groupings and cultural expressions, however, one can discern commonalities in worldviews that make it possible to speak of an "African" worldview as compared, say, to a "Hindu" one. Summarizing distinctive markers of this African worldview, Sambuli Mosha (Mosha, 2000) isolates four key ideas, namely:

30. *Wikipedia*, s.v. "Shamanism," 3. Beliefs.

31. "Shamanism Is Not a Religion," https://www.faena.com/aleph/shamanism-is-not-a-religion-but-healing-based-on-generosity.

Afterlife Beliefs

1. the centrality of belief in God

2. an acknowledgment of the intrinsic unity between individuals and communities

3. viewing the universe as an interconnected, interdependent whole

4. embracing life as a process of spiritual formation and transformation

All these markers shape the way Africans conceptualize both this life and the hereafter.

Secondly, African beliefs are dynamic rather than static. They are shaped and influenced by other belief systems that they encounter in history. While this dynamism is manifest in all aspects of belief, here we focus on concepts of the hereafter. In this regard, we note for example that ancient Egyptians held very clear eschatological ideas featuring notions of heaven and hell and a final judgment. Thus, in the Egyptian *Book of the Dead*, a text designed to be a guide for the soul as it journeyed on beyond physical death, Osiris determines the destiny of the dead. Having measured their moral worth against the feather of Maat (symbolizing truth and justice), he sends them "west," to the "abode of the righteous," or to "hell." Today, the pyramids where the pharaohs, ancient Egyptian kings believed to be immortal, were entombed remain an enduring testimony of the ancient Egyptians' preoccupation with life after death.

Two thousand years later, these Egyptian ideas of the hereafter were part of the repertoire of beliefs in circulation in the Mediterranean world as Christianity was taking shape. Later still, in the nineteenth century, through Christian missionaries these ideas found their way into sub-Saharan Africa. Here, they reinforced prior indigenous concepts of the afterlife where these were already incorporated notions of a final judgment, as in the case of the Yoruba of Nigeria and LoDagaa of Ghana (Ray, 1976, pp. 143ff). Elsewhere, for example among the Agikuyu of Kenya, ideas of heaven and hell were introduced de novo, since this community's prior concepts of the hereafter had no such notions. Among the Gikuyu, as was typical in most indigenous African communities, though one's moral misconduct could provoke divine anger and punishment, such punishment was this-worldly rather than delayed and otherworldly.[32]

---

32. *Encyclopedia.com*, s.v. "Afterlife: African Concepts."

Appendix B

Traditional Africans believe in a life after death for their ancestors but are not aware of rewards or punishment in the afterlife (Mbiti 1975a:259–62; 1985:161; Sundermeier 1990:154; Hammond-Tooke 1993:149). Theo Sundermeier (1990:154, 201), however, notes two exceptions. The Koko and Basa peoples of Cameroon believe that evil people are destined for a cold place and good people for a place full of light. In view of the fact that they also believe that the repenters are destined for an intermediate state of existence, the originality of their beliefs is, however, doubtful. The Akan people of Ghana (according to Sundermeier) is the other exception. They believe in reward and punishment after life. The rest of Africa believes in a God that judges and punishes evildoers in the here and now during their earthly life, but not after death. John Mbiti (1975a:259–62; 1985:161) also refers to some exceptions to the rule. In this regard he mentions the Yoruba who believe in a judgment after death, based on earthly morality and the Lodagaa who fear punishment of evil by the ancestors after death. He also refers to, the Lozi who believe that eternal life (or life with the ancestors) will only be granted when people could identify themselves to the ancestors through tribal marks on their arms. Therefore, as far as we know this epithet of God is, apart from these exceptions, unknown to traditional Africa. Steve Biko (2004:49) affirms this when he, as a Christian traditionalist, states:

> "We believed—and this was consistent with our views of life—that all people who died had a special place next to God. We felt that a communication with God could only be through these people. We never knew anything about hell—we do not believe that God can create people only to punish them eternally after a short period on earth . . . It was the missionaries who confused our people with their religion. They . . . preach a theology of the existence of hell, scaring our fathers and mothers with stories about burning in eternal flames and gnashing of teeth and grinding of bone. This cold cruel religion was strange to us but our fore-fathers [sic!] were sufficiently scared of the unknown impending [d]anger to believe that it was worth a try. Down went our cultural values!"[33]

It is not widely realized, however, that reincarnation is an essential tenet of many traditional African religious systems and philosophies. Belief in rebirth has been reported amongst peoples

---

33. Van Wyk, "African Traditional Religion."

scattered the length and breadth of the mighty continent: Akamba (Kenya), Akan (Ghana), Lango (Uganda), Luo (Zambia), Ndebele (Zimbabwe), Sebei (Uganda), Yoruba (Nigeria), Shona (Zimbabwe), Nupe (Nigeria), Illa (Zambia), and many others. There is, of course, a wide variation in understanding of the processes of rebirth: beliefs range from that in a "partial" reincarnation of an ancestor in one or several individuals strictly within the same family, to that in an endless cycle of rebirths linked to a notion of cleansing and refinement of the inner nature.

As there are endless shades of understanding, reincarnation is known by many names: amongst the Yorubas of Nigeria rebirth is referred to in various ways, including Yiya omo, translated as the "shooting forth of a branch" or "turning to be child," and A-tun-wa, "another coming." The Aboh-speaking peoples of the Ibo family of nations in Nigeria speak of Inua u'we or "returning to life," as they believe death is an end to one life only and a gateway to another; man must be reborn, for reincarnation is a spiritual necessity.

The ancient theosophy underlying traditional African religions becomes even more apparent as we delve into the fascinating complexities of their interpretations of the doctrine of rebirth. There seems to be a common belief amongst them that the wave of human souls at any particular world period is limited in number; therefore, reincarnation is only logical. For example, the Illa people of southern Zambia believe that a certain number of spirits were created and given bodies at the dawn of manifestation. When the bodies wear out during the course of a lifetime, the spirits live on in their own sphere of consciousness and then have other bodies prepared for them at the appropriate time. Linked with this is a belief in the inevitability of rebirth for the majority of humanity with only two exceptions cited by the Illa elders—the mizhimo or "tribal gods," and those unfortunate individuals whose spiritual evolution has in some way been interrupted by sorcerers. The Illa also believe that the reincarnating spirit is sexless and may seek manifestation in either the body of a man or woman regardless of the individual's sex in a previous life. They say, in common with the esoteric teachings of many other religious traditions, that the incarnating spirit, the true Self of each individual, provides to the newly-born child no memory of previous lives in the worlds of either spirit or matter. During life, the spirit animates the body but remains untainted by the vicissitudes of daily living. One is reminded of the ancient Greek myths regarding the river of Lethe or Forgetfulness in the Underworld, from which those about to be reincarnated drank a certain portion which made them forget their former existence.[34]

9. Sikhism

Sikhs do not believe in an afterlife in either Heaven or Hell. Sikhism teaches that the soul reincarnates when the body dies. They believe that the soul has to transmigrate from one body either human or animal to another as part of an evolution process of the soul. This evolution of the soul will eventually result in a union with God upon the proper purification of the spirit. Sikhs believe that good, or bad actions, determine the life form which a soul takes in rebirth.

At the time of death, demonic, ego centered souls may be destined to suffer great agonies, and pain, in the dark underworld of Narak. It is unknown how long a soul will remain there, but it is not thought to be permanent. Once cleansed of its misdeeds, the soul is reborn and continues its journey towards liberation. If one does not perform righteous deeds, one's soul will continue to cycle in reincarnation forever. A being who has performed good deeds and actions in their lives is transmigrated to a better and higher life form in the next life until the soul of the being becomes Godlike.

A soul, fortunate enough to achieve grace, overcomes ego by meditating on God. In Sikhism, the focus meditation is to remember the divine Enlightener by calling out the name "Waheguru (God)," either silently or aloud. Such a soul may attain liberation from the cycle of reincarnation. The soul then experiences salvation in Sachkhand, the realm of truth, where it exists eternally, as an entity of radiant light.

Bhagat Trilochan, an author of Guru Granth Sahib scripture, writes on the subject of afterlife, that at the time of death the final thought determine how one reincarnates.

"At the very last moment, one who thinks of wealth, and dies in such thoughts, shall be reincarnated in the form of serpent. One should not forget the Naam. At the very last moment, he who thinks of women, and dies in such thoughts, shall be reincarnated as a prostitute. At the very last moment, one who thinks of his children, and dies in such thoughts, shall be reincarnated as a pig. At the very last moment, one who thinks of mansions, and dies in

34. Rooke, "Reincarnation in African Religion."

such thoughts, shall be reincarnated as a goblin. At the very last moment, one who thinks of the Lord, and dies in such thoughts, says Bhagat Trilochan, that man becomes liberated and the Lord abides in his heart." (Guru Granth Sahib Ji, 526)[35]

"People continue wandering through the cycle of 8.4 million incarnations; without the true Guru, liberation is not obtained. Reading and studying, the Pandits (religious scholars) and the silent sages have grown weary, but attached to the love of duality, they have lost their honor. The true Guru teaches the word of Shabad; without the True One, there is no other at all. Those who are linked by the True One are linked to Truth. They always act in Truth." (Guru Granth Sahib Ji, 70)[36]

10. Juche ("Independent Stand" or "Self-Reliance")

Juche is the only government-recognized ideology within North Korea. Not traditionally considered a religion, but more of a combination of philosophy, educational strategy, and religious practices, Juche could be described as a nationalist, secular, ethical ideology. Juche, literally "main body," has often been translated within North Korea as meaning "independent stand" or "self-reliance." Created in 1955 by North Korean President Kim Il-Sung, traditional Juche holds that even though humanity is independent and the primary agent in its own destiny, it also contains a collective unconsciousness grounded in the "Great Leader." Juche teaches that the North Korean people need to be organized and guided by the "Great Leader," who was Kim Il-Sung himself. Many consider Juche to be a personality cult created by Il-Sung to promote himself, his family, and his ideas. As a social and political ideology, many of the components of Juche are similar to Marxism as well as some Communist ideologies of China (Maoism) and the former U.S.S.R. (Leninism). Originally constructed as an ideology to assist North Korea with its independence, Juche also claims to be an ideology to assist other developing countries with understanding and developing their true independence. Juche ideology developed further in 1994 when General Secretary Kim Jong-il, Kim Il-Sung's son and successor, added some of the

35. Khalsa, "Sikhism and the Afterlife."
36. See http://www.realsikhism.com/gurbani/popup.php?pagenumber=70_1.

ethical components of Confucianism to Juche, including doctrines addressing material possessions, family values, and self-sacrifice. Even though small pockets of Juche have developed in other countries, the great majority of Juche followers live in North Korea.[37]

The Juche religion does not advocate an official philosophy regarding life after death, or if there is such a thing. Therefore, no conclusion can be drawn regarding what its adherents believe will happen to them when they die. Research has revealed that some followers profess that upon death, they will be reunited with Kim Il-Sung and be with him forever. This cannot be generalized as an accepted belief by all Juche followers. The afterlife is simply not the focus of the religion. Its foundational premise is that man is the master of everything and decides everything; so, whatever happens after death will be decided by man.

11. Spiritism (also referred to as Spiritualism)

The spiritualist's basic view of the afterlife is one where the dead are able to watch the living from a distance, and often want to offer advice to living friends and relatives about how to solve their earthly problems. They also offer encouragement to the living about the certainty of an afterlife that is largely pleasant and satisfying, and in doing so contradict claims about the extremes of heaven and hell described in mainstream Christianity.

Spiritualism can even be viewed as a concrete alternative to Christianity because the spirits purport to offer direct evidence of an afterlife by telling the audience facts about individuals in the audience that are unknown to the spiritualist and the rest of the audience. The target individual then confirms the facts to be correct and the audience concludes that the dead are indeed speaking. If the information is wrong or irrelevant (does not apply to the target individual), the spiritualist has various excuses about how or why the information got garbled.

The spiritualist's approach usually requires no faith in God or Christ though some churches wed the two very different systems of Christianity and Spiritualism in a strange admixture of often contradictory ideas (most spiritualists believe in reincarnation). There is also no need of attaining salvation to escape hell in the afterlife. This statement that there should be no fear of hell in the afterlife generally applies to the average person who has not

37. *Patheos*, "Juche."

committed egregious evil acts during life. And even such evil do-
ers will not experience torment eternally but will eventually move
beyond it.[38]

[Spiritualism] says that all people and animals that have been
loved (had their vibrations raised) such as pets, continue to live
after physical death. On crossing over we take three things with
us: our etheric or spirit body (a duplicate of our physical body) all
memories and our character.

On crossing we go to a realm that will accommodate the vibrations we accumulated from all the thoughts and actions of our
lifetime. Average decent people go to what is usually termed as the
Third Realm. Those who have been willfully cruel and consistently
selfish go to the darker, very unpleasant Astral regions because
their level of vibrations would be much lower than the vibrations
of the Third Realm.

Information transmitted from the other side tells us that
the Third Realm is a place of enormous beauty, peace and light.
There will be scope to continue to spiritually refine indefinitely.
Those who earned it can progress to the fourth level, then the
fifth, and sixth and so on. For humans we know that there are at
least seven realms vibrating from the lowest to the highest—the
higher the vibrations the more beautiful and better the conditions.
Spiritualists accept the Law of Progress—that those who are in the
lower realms will one day slowly go upwardly towards the Realms
of the Light even if it takes eons of time.[39]

As an informal movement, Spiritualism does not have a defined
set of rules, but various Spiritualist organizations have adopted
variations on some or all of a "Declaration of Principles" developed between 1899 and 1944 and revised as recently as 2004. In
October 1899, a six article "Declaration of Principles" was adopted
by the National Spiritualist Association (NSA) at a convention in
Chicago, Illinois. Two additional principles were added by the
NSA in October 1909, at a convention in Rochester, New York.
Finally, in October 1944, a ninth principle was adopted by the Na-
tional Spiritualist Association of Churches, at a convention in St.
Louis, Missouri.[40]

38. Denosky, "Spiritualism and Spiritual Travel."
39. Zammit, "Afterlife: Spiritualism/Spiritism."
40. *Wikipedia*, s.v. "Spiritualism," 1.2.1. Declaration of Principles.

Appendix B

The National Association of Spiritualist Churches in the USA has nine principles which provide more information about Spiritualist beliefs:

1. We believe in Infinite Intelligence.

2. We believe that the phenomena of Nature, both physical and spiritual, are the expression of Infinite Intelligence.

3. We affirm that a correct understanding of such expression and living in accordance therewith, constitute true religion.

4. We affirm that the existence and personal identity of the individual continue after the change called death.

5. We affirm that communication with the so-called dead is a fact, scientifically proven by the phenomena of Spiritualism.

6. We believe that the highest morality is contained in the Golden Rule: 'Whatsoever ye would that others should do unto you do ye also unto them.' ['Do unto others as you would have them do unto you.']

7. We affirm the moral responsibility of individuals and that we make our own happiness or unhappiness as we obey or disobey Nature's physical and spiritual laws.

8. We affirm that the doorway to reformation is never closed against any soul here or hereafter.

9. We affirm that the precepts of Prophecy and Healing are Divine attributes proven through Mediumship.[41]

Spiritualism is too diverse to have a universal code of beliefs; instead, Spiritualists accept sets of more wide-ranging principles.

"We believe in freedom of religion and freedom of worship— and that you worship God in your own way. Spiritualism gives you a set of values that enables you to think about how your relationship with God should be."
—Alan Baker, President of the Havant Spiritualist Church

The Spiritualists' National Union in the UK bases itself on the Seven Principles, which all full members must accept. These are:

1. The Fatherhood of God

2. The Brotherhood of Man

41. BBC, "Religions: Declaration of Principles."

3. The Communion of Spirits and the Ministry of Angels

4. The continuous existence of the human soul

5. Personal responsibility

6. Compensation and retribution hereafter for all the good and evil deeds done on earth

7. Eternal progress open to every human soul[42]

12. Judaism

When examining Jewish intellectual sources throughout history, there is clearly a spectrum of opinions regarding death versus the afterlife. In the biblical text of Psalms, there is a description of death, when people go into the earth or the "realm of the dead" and cannot praise God. The first reference to resurrection is collective in Ezekiel's vision of the dry bones, when all the Israelites in exile will be resurrected. There is a reference to individual resurrection in the Book of Daniel (165 B.C.E.), the last book of the Hebrew Bible [as ordered in the Old Testament].

During the Second Temple Period, the Sadducees, High Priests, denied any particular existence of individuals after death because it wasn't written in the Torah, while the Pharisees, ancestors of the rabbis, affirmed both bodily resurrection and immortality of the soul, most likely based on the influence of Hellenistic ideas about body and soul and the Pharisaic belief in the Oral Torah. The Pharisees maintained that after death, the soul is connected to God until the messianic era when it is rejoined with the body in the land of Israel at the time of resurrection.

Sadducees (High Priests)	Pharisees (Ancestors of Rabbis)
Deny existence after death	Affirm bodily resurrection and immortality of the soul
	Body and soul rejoined in messianic era

According to various Jewish intellectual sources and folk traditions up through the medieval period, there is a gradual transition from physical death to an afterlife in which the body

42. BBC, "Religions: Beliefs."

and spirit remain connected to one another in some way either through resurrection or immortality of the soul. According to early rabbinic folklore, the transition from death to life actually begins three days after death when the soul is believed to hover over the grave hoping to be restored to the body. Yet some rabbinic sources claim that twelve months after death, the soul maintains a temporary relationship with body in a type of purgatory leading either to paradise, Gan Eden, or hell, Gehinnom.

The condition of the soul during the twelve-month purgatory is uncertain. There is a spectrum of opinions ranging from the idea that it is quiescent to fully conscious with the only difference being the power of speech. There is also a debate about how much the dead know of the world left behind. The rabbis even decried the practice of eating a meal between Shabbat afternoon prayers and sunset because of God's custom of letting spirits out of their storage place and giving them food from the "courtyard of the dead" and brook water flowing out of the Garden of Eden.

According to medieval folklore, there was a belief in the spirits of the deceased maintaining bodily form in a ghostly existence and tormenting the living. There was actually a popular belief that ghosts gathered nightly with other spirits, studying, adjudicating disputes, and praying. In this interaction between spiritual and earthly realms, ghosts met during the day while carrying out a punishment on earth or told survivors about good fortune in olam ha-bah, the "World to Come." One could even argue that there was interdependence between the dead and living with the former being given food and water by the latter during Shabbat.

In medieval philosophical sources, Rabbi Saadiah Gaon (892–942) promoted a belief in bodily resurrection based on the argument of God's status as creator. He argued that if God could create the world out of nothing, then all the more so can God "create something from something disintegrated and dissolved," in other words, refashioning and reviving the dead. Maimonides (1135–1204) rejected bodily resurrection in favor of immortality of the soul based on neo-Platonic and Aristotelian denigration of the body. He argued that literal understandings of bodily resurrection are naïve and based on the immaturity of the masses who must be encouraged to obey God's commandments in order to receive some physical reward or induce fear of receiving punishment. In reality, according to Maimonides, the soul continues on after the death of the body, experiencing eternal pleasures of the spirit. He based this on a Talmudic passage from Brachot 17a, "In the world to come there is no eating, drinking, washing, anointing or sexual intercourse, but the righteous sit with their crowns on their heads enjoying the radiance of the Divine Presence."[43]

In rabbinic literature, there are sources on divine judgment and salvation in olam ha-bah, the "World to Come." Divine judgment of the wicked occurs in Gehenna or Gehennom, a type of purgatory or hell where they will be cleansed of their sins for up to a year and beyond. Salvation in olam ha-bah is described in three different ways: disembodied souls basking in the divine presence with no bodily urges; feasting out of the flesh of Leviathan; and generally experiencing eternal life with no evil.[44]

Finally, according to the rabbis, both the Jews and righteous Gentiles will receive salvation in olam ha-bah. Jewish people have a "reserved place" in olam ha-bah based on their study of Torah along with prayer, repentance, and good deeds, though their "reservation" for olam ha-bah can be cancelled as a result of sins. The rabbis also gleaned from the Torah that there are seven universal commandments enjoined to the children of Noah. Because they saw their interpretations as an extension of divine revelation through the Oral Torah, the rabbis believed that these commandments were actually given by God, even though they are not explicitly stated in the Torah. According to the rabbis, righteous Gentiles are eligible to receive salvation based on whether they have fulfilled these seven commandments: to establish courts of justice and to refrain from blaspheming the God of Israel, idolatry, sexual perversion, bloodshed, robbery, and eating meat cut from a living animal. Ultimately, as indicated in the Hebrew Scriptures and reiterated by post-Holocaust theologian Irving Greenberg, it was always God's plan to bring redemption to both Jews and the non-Jewish world.[45]

Traditional Judaism firmly believes that death is not the end of human existence. However, because Judaism is primarily focused on life here and now rather than on the afterlife, Judaism does not have much dogma about the afterlife, and leaves a great deal of room for one's personal opinion. It is possible for an Orthodox Jew to believe that the souls of the righteous dead go to a place similar to the Christian heaven, or that they are reincarnated through

43. *Patheos*, "Judaism," §Beliefs: Afterlife and Salvation.
44. *Patheos*, "Judaism," §Beliefs: Afterlife and Salvation.
45. *Patheos*, "Judaism," §Beliefs: Afterlife and Salvation.

many lifetimes, or that they simply wait until the coming of the messiah, when they will be resurrected. Likewise, Orthodox Jews can believe that the souls of the wicked are tormented by demons of their own creation, or that wicked souls are simply destroyed at death, ceasing to exist.[46]

Traditional Judaism teaches that after death our bodies go to the grave, but our souls go before God to be judged. God, as He states in Scripture, is the only one who knows our motives as well as our works—God sees the heart, whereas man looks at the outside (1 Samuel 16:7). Facing the only true Judge, we are assigned a place in heaven according to a merit system based on God's accounting of all our actions and motives. Traditional Jewish thought is that only the very righteous go directly to heaven; all others must be cleansed of residual sin.

According to traditional Judaism, sins that were not cleansed prior to death are removed after death in a place called Sheol or Gehinnom (also spelled Gehinom and Gehenna). The name of the place is taken from a valley (Gei Hinnom) just south of Jerusalem, once used for child sacrifice by the pagan nations of Canaan (2 Kings 23:10). Some Jews view Gehinnom as a place of torture and punishment, fire and brimstone. Others imagine it less harshly, as a place where one reviews the actions of his or her life and repents for past misdeeds. "Hell" in Judaism is a place where the soul is cleansed or refined (see Zechariah 13:9). The exceedingly righteous and those who repent before they die can avoid being "cleansed" in hell. This doctrine bears some similarity to the Catholic teaching of Purgatory.

Contrary to the Christian view of eternal damnation in Hades or hell, the "punishment" of Sheol is temporary. Judaism bases its doctrine of a temporary hell on Psalm 16:10, 1 Samuel 2:6, and Jonah 2:3. According to rabbinic teachings, the soul's sentence in Gehinnom is usually limited to a twelve-month period of purgation before the soul takes its place in *Olam Ha-Ba* (Mishnah Eduyot 2:9, Shabbat 33a). This twelve-month limit is reflected in the year-long mourning cycle and the recitation of the *kaddish*, the memorial prayer for the dead. Second Temple Judaism believed that, until the Messiah came, it was not possible for the faithful to enter heaven. They remained in Sheol, waiting.

In the Jewish view of hell, the pain the soul experiences is not physical; rather, it is psychological anguish—the shame and

46. Zammit, "Afterlife: Judaism."

disgrace one feels upon reviewing one's personal history of life in a body and seeing how many opportunities to serve God were wasted. Almost everyone, including non-Jewish people, can merit a portion in the World to Come. But some will not be given a chance of heaven: "Multitudes who sleep in the dust of the earth will awake: some to everlasting life, others to shame and everlasting contempt" (Daniel 12:2). The "everlasting contempt," in the Jewish view, is reserved for completely evil, unredeemable people such as King Ahab, the men of Sodom, and Adolf Hitler.

Just as all Christians do not agree on eschatology, all Jewish people do not agree on the afterlife. What the Bible clearly teaches is that sin demands a price to be paid by someone, there is an afterlife, and, in Christ, both Jews and Gentiles can have a place in Olam Ha-Ba, the World to Come.[47]

13. Bahá'í

The Bahá'í scriptures assert that there is life after death; indeed, the whole purpose of human life in this world is a preparation for that life. Human beings have only one lifetime on this earth and the purpose of this life is to acquire spiritual virtues [kindness, generosity, integrity, truthfulness, humility, and selfless service to others] in preparation for the next life, which is a purely spiritual life, and so these spiritual virtues will only fully come into their own in that next life.

The Bahá'í scriptures teach that human life in this world is like that of the embryo in the womb, which is developing arms, legs, eyes, and ears that are of little use in that world of the uterus. It is only when it dies to that world and is born into this world that it is able to use these organs fully. Similarly, human beings are instructed by the Manifestations of God to develop certain virtues. Humans cannot entirely understand the reason for this now but if they were to fail to develop these virtues, they would be born into the next world handicapped, just as an embryo that fails to develop arms or legs or eyes is handicapped when it is born into this world.[48]

---

47. "Do Jews Believe in Hell?," https://www.gotquestions.org/do-Jews-believe-in-hell.html.

48. *Patheos*, "Baha'i," §Beliefs: Afterlife and Salvation.

Appendix B

According to the Bahá'í scriptures, human beings have neither the vocabulary to discuss nor the conceptual ability to understand the spiritual world that permeates this reality and to which humans go after death. It is therefore only possible to speak of it in terms of metaphors and analogies such as the one above. In general, however, these scriptures portray a picture of gradual spiritual progress after death attaining, eventually, the presence of God. Part of the reason that the nature of the afterlife is hidden from humans may be because, as Baha'u'llah states, if humans were to understand its nature, they could not bear to remain in this world. It is for this reason that Baha'u'llah writes that He has made death a "messenger of joy" and that human beings should not fear death. Suicide, however, is prohibited in the Bahá'í Faith.

The souls of those who have died can have a positive influence on this physical world, encouraging the progress and advancement of the people of this world. According to the Bahá'í teachings, however, there is no evil influence from the souls of those who have died; because of their spiritual disabilities, evil souls have no ability to influence this world. Bahá'ís are also discouraged from trying to contact the dead (for example, through mediums). This is an obstacle to the spiritual development of both those who are alive and those who are dead.

There is no concept of a state of salvation in the Bahá'í teachings; rather salvation is a process. The process of acquiring spiritual virtues makes us more and more fit to enter the next world. The main aim of life should be to perfect these spiritual attributes; the more these are perfected, the closer humans become to God. And it is this closeness to God that is the heaven or paradise referred to in the scriptures of all religions. Failing to develop these virtues means humans separating themselves from God, and that is hell. Thus, heaven and hell are not distinct places; they are spiritual conditions both in this world and in the afterlife. Human progress along this path occurs partly as the result of the individual's own efforts and partly due to the grace of God during this life. After death, progress is mostly from the grace of God, but human beings can assist this progress by praying for those who have died.[49]

A consequence of holding to this view of salvation as a process is that human beings are in no position to judge each other. A person may appear to be very far advanced on the spiritual road, but may be traveling very slowly or have stopped, and is thus

---

49. *Patheos*, "Baha'i," §Beliefs: Afterlife and Salvation.

blameworthy in the sight of God. Another person may not appear to be very advanced but may be making rapid progress. Furthermore, Baha'u'llah warns that it is even possible at the hour of death for someone to gain faith and attain a high spiritual station and conversely for another to lose faith and fall from a high spiritual station to a low one.[50]

14. Jainism

Jains believe in cycling through birth and rebirth. However, their take on things is a little different from most religions that believe this. Not only can you be reincarnated into the earthly realm, but also into their layers of heaven and hells. You are not permanently stuck in hell, once you die there, you may be reincarnated back into the earthly realm. Where you go depends on your karma. Moksha (the end of the cycling through birth and rebirth) comes when one finds enlightenment, like the tirthankaras. In addition, you cannot attain Moksha until you have been a man in at least one of your lives.

The layers of heaven and hell consist of . . .

1. The supreme abode: This is located at the top of the universe and is where Siddha, the liberated souls, live.

2. The upper world: 30 heavens where celestial beings live.

3. Middle world: the earth and the rest of the universe.

4. Nether world: 7 hells with various levels of misery and punishments.

5. The Nigoda, or base: where the lowest forms of life reside.

6. Universe space: layers of clouds which surround the upper world.

7. Space beyond: an infinite volume without soul, matter, time, medium of motion or medium.[51]

In Jainism, godliness is said to be the inherent quality of every soul. This quality, however, is subdued by the soul's association with karmic matter. All souls who have achieved the natural state

50. *Patheos*, "Baha'i," §Beliefs: Afterlife and Salvation.

51. "What Is the Afterlife of Jainism?," https://www.answers.com/Q/What_is_the_afterlife_of_jainism.

of infinite bliss, infinite knowledge (kevala jnana), infinite power and infinite perception are regarded as God in Jainism. Jainism rejects the idea of a creator deity responsible for the manifestation, creation, or maintenance of this universe. According to Jain doctrine, the universe and its constituents (soul, matter, space, time, and principles of motion) have always existed. All the constituents and actions are governed by universal natural laws and perfect soul, an immaterial entity cannot create or affect a material entity like the universe.[52]

Jain ideas about the soul differ from those of many other religions.
The Jain word that comes closest to soul is jiva, which means a conscious, living being. For Jains body and soul are different things: the body is just an inanimate container—the conscious being is the jiva.

After each bodily death, the jiva is reborn into a different body to live another life, until it achieves liberation. When a jiva is embodied (i.e., in a body), it exists throughout that body and isn't found in any particular bit of it.

Jains believe:

- the soul exists forever

- each soul is always independent

- the soul is responsible for what it does

- the soul experiences the consequences of its actions

- the soul can become liberated from the cycle of birth and death

- not all souls can be liberated—some souls are inherently incapable of achieving this

- the soul can evolve towards that liberation by following principles of behaviour[53]

15. Shinto ("the Way of *Kami*" or "Way of the Gods")

"There is an old saying in Japan: 'born Shinto, die Buddhist.' Before Buddhism, it was believed that all who died went to a vast hellish underworld from which there is no escape. Buddhism introduced the idea of rewards

52. *Wikipedia*, s.v. "God in Jainism."
53. *BBC*, "Religions: The Soul."

and punishments in the afterlife, and death and salvation in the afterlife came to be regarded as Buddhist matters."[54]

The afterlife is not a primary concern in Shinto.

Shinto is a difficult religion to classify. On the one hand, it can be seen as merely a highly sophisticated form of animism and may be regarded as a primal religion. On the other hand, Shinto beliefs and ways of thinking are deeply embedded in the subconscious fabric of modern Japanese society. The afterlife is not a primary concern in Shinto, and much more emphasis is placed on fitting into this world, instead of preparing for the next. Shinto has no binding set of dogma, no holiest place for worshippers, no person or kami deemed holiest, and no defined set of prayers. Instead, Shinto is a collection of rituals and methods meant to mediate the relations of living humans to kami. These practices have originated organically in Japan over a span of many centuries and have been influenced by Japan's contact with the religions of other nations, especially China. (Notice that the word Shinto is itself of Chinese origin.) Conversely, Shinto had and continues to have an impact of the practice of other religions within Japan. In particular, one could even make a case for discussing it under the heading of Japanese Buddhism, since these two religions have exercised a profound influence on each other throughout Japanese history. The Japanese "New religions" that have emerged since the end of the Second World War also show a clear Shinto influence.

Shinto has no absolute commandments for its adherents outside of living "a simple and harmonious life with nature and people." Because Shinto has co-existed with Buddhism for well over a millennium, it is very difficult to disentangle Shinto and Buddhist beliefs about the world. One might say that where Buddhism emphasizes the afterlife and ending the cycle of rebirths, Shinto emphasizes this life and finding happiness within it.[55]

Shinto traditions lean heavily on the concepts of the presence of kami and not reincarnation. The spiritual energy, or kami, in everyone is released and recycled at the time of death. The spirits live in another world, the most sacred of which is called "the other world of heaven." These other worlds are not seen as a paradise or a punishment. Instead the worlds are simply where the spirits

---

54. *Patheos*, "Shinto," §Beliefs: Afterlife and Salvation.

55. "What Is the Shintoism Belief about Afterlife?," https://answers.yahoo.com/question/index?qid=20081108090138AAnFvwn.

reside. They can connect and visit the present world when people correctly perform rituals and festivals.

Shinto believes that the ancestral spirits will protect their descendants. The prayers and rituals performed by the living honor the dead and memorialize them. In return, the spirits of the dead offer protection and encouragement for the living.

Shintoism also views that some individuals live such an exemplary life that they become deified in a process called apotheosis. Many in the imperial family have experienced this honor, as have successful warriors.[56]

"There is no concept of an eternal soul in Shinto."[57]

16. Cao Dai ("Highest Lord" or "Highest Power")

In Cao Dai, the purpose of life is peace within each individual and harmony in the world. Cao Dai followers also seek to gain religious merit and avoid bad karma.

Cao Dai beliefs about the afterlife are derived from Buddhism. Those who have gathered too much bad karma during their lifetime will be reincarnated in negative circumstances, which may include rebirth on a darker, colder planet than this one. Good karma leads to rebirth to a better life on earth.

Salvation is freedom from rebirth and the attainment of nirvana or heaven. "The ultimate goal of Cao Daists is to be reunified with The All That Is, to return home."[58]

17. Zoroastrianism

The Zoroastrian afterlife is determined by the balance of the good and evil deeds, words, and thoughts of the whole life. For those whose good deeds outweigh the bad, heaven awaits. Those who did more evil than good go to hell (which has several levels

56. "Understanding Shinto: After Life," https://www.econdolence.com/learning-center/religion-and-culture/shinto/understanding-shinto/.

57. Horton, "Shinto."

58. "Cao Dai: Beliefs," https://religionfacts.com/cao-dai/beliefs.

corresponding to degrees of wickedness). There is an intermediate stage for those whose deeds weight out equally.

This general principle is not absolute, however, but allows for human weakness. All faults do not have to be registered or weighed forever on the scales. There are two means of effacing them: confession and the transfer of supererogatory merits (similar to the Roman Catholic "Treasury of Merits"). The latter is the basis for Zoroastrian prayers and ceremonies for the departed.[59]

Consequently very influential ideas about the afterlife—like hell, heaven, individual judgment, resurrection of the dead, and last judgment—might originate here, or they might be later borrowings. We find the idea of the judgment of the individual at death as an element of the Egyptian afterlife, but there is no evidence of Egyptian influence on the ideas of Zoroastrianism. Zoroastrianism probably does introduce the idea of final judgment or Apocalypse (Frashegird or Frashokereti). The fate of wicked souls after the Frashgird evolved in Zoroastrianism. Scholars of Zoroastrianism find that in earlier texts, the souls would be subjected to everlasting punishment in hell, later the belief was that they would be destroyed in the molten metal of the Apocalypse, and even later belief holds that the molten metal will actually purify everything, allowing even the wicked to proceed to heaven. However, the ultimate fate of the wicked is not conclusively explained in any of the hell texts themselves.[60]

Even among Zoroastrian holy texts, you'll find only a few overt mentions of the nature of Hell, but the Book of Arda Viraf describes the Zoroastrian Hell as a place of fire with a terrible stench. Further description divides this Hell into different regions such as the place of evil deeds and the place of evil words. In another reference in the book translated as Religious Judgments, the deepest pit of Hell is described as a place so dark that it is as if the people sent there are blind. The Zoroastrian Hell, however, is not eternal and at the end of the world God will purify all souls.[61]

59. "Zoroastrianism: Zoroastrian Beliefs," https://religionfacts.com/zoroastrianism/beliefs.

60. Gardiner, "About Zoroastrian Hell."

61. Stuart, "Zoroastrians on Hell."

18. Tenrikyo ("Religion of Divine Wisdom")

Tenrikyo affirms the concept of reincarnation, where the soul continually returns into the world with a new biological life after the death of the previous one. Reincarnation also appears in Indian religions such as Hinduism, Buddhism and Jainism.

Tenrikyo's understanding of reincarnation is referred to as *denaoshi* (出直し, "to make a fresh start"). *Denaoshi* is related to the teaching of a thing lent, a thing borrowed, in that when a person's physical body dies, the soul is returning to God the body that has been borrowed from God. This allows the soul to accept a new body to be lent by God and thus reenter the physical world. Though the reborn person has no memory of the previous life, the person's thoughts and deeds leave their mark on the soul and are carried over into the new life as the person's causality (see section on causality).

Nakayama Miki taught that the process of *denaoshi* is like taking off old clothes in order to put on new ones, an image that emphasizes the materiality of the body. Human beings are given countless opportunities to realize the world of the Joyous Life (the state of salvation) in this world, as opposed to another realm in the afterlife such as heaven.[62]

"The goal of Tenrikyō is a happy life free from disease and suffering. The modern sect emphasizes modern medical care. The centre of religious activity is the *jiba*, a sacred recess in the sanctuary of the main temple in Tenri city (Nara Prefecture). The world is said to have been created here, and from the *jiba* salvation will finally be extended to the entire world."[63]

19. Neopaganism

"Neopaganism is not an organized religion and has no official doctrine. Pagans follow a wide variety of paths and may have a variety of beliefs on religious questions like the divine, human nature and the afterlife. However, there are some common beliefs that are held by most Neopagans."[64]

The common portrayal of the Summerland is as a place of rest for souls in between their earthly incarnations.

62. *Wikipedia*, s.v. "Tenrikyo Anthropology," 2. Rebirth.
63. *Britannica.com*, s.v. "Tenrikyō."
64. "Neopagan Beliefs," https://religionfacts.com/neopaganism/beliefs.

In Theosophy, the term "Summerland" is used without the definite article "the." Summerland, also called the Astral plane Heaven, is depicted as where souls who have been good in their previous lives go between incarnations.

Theosophists believe the Summerlands are maintained by hosts of planetary angels serving Sanat Kumara, the Nordic alien from Venus who Theosophists believe is the governing deity of Earth and leader of the Spiritual Hierarchy of Earth. Sanat Kumara is believed to rule over our planet from the floating city of Shamballa, believed by Theosophists to exist on the etheric plane (a plane between the physical plane and the astral plane), about five miles (8 km) above the Gobi Desert.

Theosophists also believe there is another higher level of heaven called Devachan, also called the Mental plane Heaven, which some but not all souls reach between incarnations—only those souls that are more highly developed spiritually reach this level, i.e., those souls that are at the first, second, and third levels of initiation.

The final permanent eternal afterlife heaven to which Theosophists believe most people will go millions or billions of years in the future, after our cycle of reincarnations in this Round is over, is called Nirvana, and is located beyond this physical Cosmos. In order to attain Nirvana, it is necessary to have attained the fourth level of initiation or higher, meaning one is an *arhat* and thus no longer needs to reincarnate.[65]

"Many believe in reincarnation after some rest and recovery in the 'Otherworld.' There is generally no concept of hell as a place of punishment, but some believe wrongdoing can trap the soul in a state of suffering after death. Some (Wicca) believe the soul joins their dead ancestors who watch over and protect their family. Some believe that life energy continues in some, if unknown, form. Some believe in various spiritual resting places. Many say we don't or can't know what happens after death."[66]

20. Unitarian Universalism

Unitarian Universalism (UU) is a liberal religion characterized by a "free and responsible search for truth and meaning." Unitarian Universalists assert no creed, but instead are unified by their

---

65. *Wikipedia*, s.v. "The Summerland," 2. Theosophy.
66. *Beliefnet*, "What Neo-Pagans Believe," §After Death.

shared search for spiritual growth, guided by a dynamic, "living tradition." Currently, these traditions are summarized by the Six Sources and Seven Principles of Unitarian Universalism, documents recognized by all congregations who choose to be a part of the Unitarian Universalist Association. These documents are 'living', meaning always open for revisiting and reworking. Unitarian Universalist (U.U.) congregations include many atheists, agnostics, and theists within their membership—and there are U.U. churches, fellowships, congregations, and societies all over America—as well as others around the world. The roots of Unitarian Universalism lie in liberal Christianity, specifically Unitarianism and universalism. Unitarian Universalists state that from these traditions comes a deep regard for intellectual freedom and inclusive love. Congregations and members seek inspiration and derive insight from all major world religions.

The beliefs of individual Unitarian Universalists range widely, including atheism, agnosticism, pantheism, panentheism, pandeism, deism, humanism, Judaism, Christianity, Islam, Hinduism, Sikhism, Buddhism, Taoism, syncretism, Omnism, Neopaganism and the teachings of the Bahá'í Faith.

The Unitarian Universalist Association (UUA) was formed in 1961 through the consolidation of the American Unitarian Association, established in 1825, and the Universalist Church of America, established in 1793. The UUA is headquartered in Boston, Massachusetts, and serves churches mostly in the United States. A group of thirty Philippine congregations is represented as a sole member within the UUA. The Canadian Unitarian Council (CUC) became an independent body in 2002. The UUA and CUC are, in turn, two of the seventeen members of the International Council of Unitarians and Universalists.[67]

"In keeping with the tradition's theological diversity, Unitarian Universalists believe in everything from heaven to reincarnation to the continuation of the dead in the memories of those still living, among other possibilities."[68]

"While there are a variety of views of the afterlife, most Unitarian Universalists consider this life the important one. Some believe in an ultimate unification with God, or the universe. Many Unitarian Universalists believe that the only afterlife is the legacy people leave on earth. Consistent with the idea of universal salvation, hell is rarely discussed except as a metaphor, as in 'hell on earth.'

67. *Wikipedia*, s.v. "Unitarian Universalism."
68. *Patheos*, "Unitarian-Universalism," §Beliefs: Afterlife and Salvation.

"Salvation receives little attention in Unitarian Universalism, but when it does, it is often construed as wholeness and health in this life, rather than a state attained after death."[69]

Christian universalism is a school of Christian theology focused around the doctrine of universal reconciliation—the view that all human beings will ultimately be "saved" and restored to a right relationship with God. *Christian universalism* and *the belief or hope in the universal reconciliation through Christ* can even be understood as synonyms.

The term *Christian universalism* was used in the 1820s by Russell Streeter of the *Christian Intelligencer* of Portland—a descendant of Adams Streeter who had founded one of the first Universalist Churches on September 14, 1785. Christian universalists believe this was the most common interpretation of Christianity in Early Christianity, prior to the 6th century. Christians from a diversity of denominations and traditions believe in the tenets of Christian universalism, such as the reality of an afterlife without the possibility of eternal punishment in hell.

As a formal Christian denomination, Christian universalism originated in the late 18th century with the Universalist Church of America. There is currently no single denomination uniting Christian universalists, but a few denominations teach some of the principles of Christian universalism or are open to them. In 2007, the Christian Universalist Association was founded to serve as an ecumenical umbrella organization for churches, ministries, and individuals who believe in Christian universalism.

Unitarian Universalism historically grew out of Christian universalism but is not an exclusively Christian denomination. It formed from a 1961 merger of two historically Christian denominations, the Universalist Church of America and the American Unitarian Association, both based in the United States.[70]

21. Rastafarianism

Rastafari has been characterized as a millenarianist movement, for it espouses the idea that the present age will come to an apocalyptic end. With Babylon destroyed, Rastas believe that humanity will be ushered into a "new age." In the 1980s, Rastas believed that this

69. Unitarian Universalist Association, "Leader Resource 3," §Afterlife.
70. *Wikipedia*, s.v. "Christian Universalism."

would happen around the year 2000. In this Day of Judgement, Babylon will be overthrown, and Rastas would be the chosen few who survive. A common view in the Rasta community was that the world's white people would wipe themselves out through nuclear war, with black Africans then ruling the world, something that they argue is prophesied in Daniel 2:31–32. In Rasta belief, the end of this present age would be followed by a millennium of peace, justice, and happiness in Ethiopia. The righteous will live in paradise in Africa. Those who had supported Babylon will be denied access to paradise. The Rasta conception of salvation has similarities with that promoted in Judaism.

Rastas do not believe that there is a specific afterlife to which human individuals go following bodily death. They believe in the possibility of eternal life, and that only those who shun righteousness will actually die. One Rasta view is that those who are righteous are believed to go through a process of reincarnation, with an individual's identity remaining throughout each of their incarnations. Barrett observed some Jamaican Rastas who believed that those Rastas who did die had not been faithful to Jah (God). He suggested that this attitude stemmed from the large numbers of young people that were then members of the movement, and who had thus seen only few Rastas die. In keeping with their views on death, Rastas eschew celebrating physical death and often avoid funerals, also repudiating the practice of ancestor veneration that is common among African traditional religions.[71]

"They [Rastafarians] believe that there is no afterlife and that a select few will be able to life forever (known to Rastas as 'Everliving') in their current physical bodies or their spiritual body. They also believe that heaven and Jah is on earth and is not separate from earth, so to live forever they must find God and heaven on earth."[72]

"Ethiopia, specifically, Africa in general, is considered the Rastas' heaven on earth. There is no afterlife or hell as Christianity believes. Rastas believe that Jah will send the signal and help the blacks exodus back to Ethiopian, their homeland. Any news from Ethiopia was taken very seriously as a warning to get ready to leave. The belief stems from Marcus Garvey's theme, 'Back to Africa.' Although Selassie's death came before this

71. *Wikipedia*, s.v. "Rastafari," 2.3. Afrocentrism and Views on Race: Salvation and Paradise.

72. "What Do Rastafarians Believe about the Afterlife?," https://www.answers.com/Q/What_do_rastafarians_believe_about_the_afterlife.

was possible, it did succeed in turning blacks desire to look towards Africa as their roots."[73]

"Rastafarians believe in physical immortality as a part of their religious doctrines. They believe that after their God has called the Day of Judgment, they will go to what they describe as Mount Zion in Africa to live in freedom forever. Instead of having everlasting life, which implies an end in the word last, the Rastas look forward to having ever living life."[74]

> Rastafarians believe reincarnation follows death and that life is eternal. People of other religions believe that once your physical body dies, you can return to Earth as another person or even as an animal. This is called reincarnation. The second after you die, you could be coming out of the womb to begin a new life. You could be reincarnated as a tree, a dog, or a wombat. Unfortunately, you'd never really know if you were reincarnated until someone very trustworthy told you. Most Rastafarian[s] believe that Selassie is in some way a reincarnation of Jesus and that the Rastafarian is the true Israelites. Rastas are physical immortalists who believe the chosen few will continue to live forever in their current bodies. This idea of ever living (rather than everlasting) life is very strong and important.[75]

> True Rastas are believed to be immortal, both physically and spiritually, a concept called "ever living." In keeping with a philosophy that celebrates life, many Rastafarians deny the possibility of death, except as a consequence of sin, and believe that the doctrine of the existence of, and reward in, the afterlife is the White man's teaching aimed at deflecting Blacks from the pursuit of their just rewards in this life. Selassie and Garvey were both adherents of Christianity oddly enough and Rastafarianism is suffused with Christian imagery. "We believe in Jesus but not the Jesus that you have to know to go to Heaven or Hell." In fact, Rastafarians traditionally view Africa, specifically Ethiopia, as heaven on earth. They do not believe in the Christian afterlife of Heaven or Hell. "We see Jesus more for the things that he taught," says Knight, "instead of focusing on Heaven or Hell as your salvation."[76]

73. *Meta-Religion*, s.v. "The Rastafarian Religion," https://www.meta-religion.com/World_Religions/Other_religions/rastafarian_religion.htm.

74. "Life after Death: Rastafari," https://death.findyourfate.com/life-after-death/rastafari.html.

75. "Life after Death: Rastafari."

76. "Life after Death: Rastafari."

22. Scientology

For Scientologists, the true self is the spirit, the thetan, the eternal essence of each individual. For millions and millions of years prior to this life, the thetan has existed and inhabited numerous bodies. This process of moving on and being reborn as a baby in a new body, called reincarnation or rebirth in some eastern religions, occurs as a natural and normal part of the universe. Scientology's understanding of the process of moving on to a next life is quite in accord with Hinduism in many respects. It would resonate with the image in the Bhagavadgita of dying as analogous to someone shedding clothing (the body) and putting on new clothing (a new body). At the same time, it also differs in important respects from eastern ideas. For example, there is no belief in karma nor is the thetan seen as experiencing any kind of moral judgment between lives that has any role in determining its next incarnation. Also, Scientologists reject any notion that a thetan would be reincarnated as an animal or in any state less than human.[77]

Singer Isaac Hayes died on Sunday [August 10, 2008] at the age of 65. Besides being a sex symbol, a soul-music legend, and a beloved voice-over artist, Hayes was also a dedicated Scientologist. According to his religious beliefs, what happens to Hayes now that he's passed away?

His soul will be "born again into the flesh of another body," as the Scientology Press Office's FAQ puts it. The actual details of how that rebirth occurs are not fully understood by church outsiders, but some core beliefs of Scientology are that every human being is really an immortal spiritual being known as a thetan and that the "meat bodies" we inhabit are merely vessels we shed upon death. (Members of the elite church cadre known as Seg Org, for example, sign contracts that pledge a billion years of service throughout successive lives.)

When a body dies, its thetan forgets the details of the former life, though painful and traumatic images known as engrams remain rooted in its unconscious. In order to move up the path of spiritual progression—known as the Bridge to Total Freedom—one must eradicate these psychic scars, which cause a person to act fearfully and irrationally. Once a Scientologist has purged them through the counseling process known as auditing, he or she is said to be "clear."

77. *Patheos*, "Scientology: Afterlife."

Afterlife Beliefs

According to an avowed Scientology antagonist who claims, on her Web site, to present factual information typically omitted from church press materials, the official Scientology publication *Celebrity* announced that Hayes attained "clear" status around 2002, though it is not known whether he progressed onto the highest parts of the Bridge, the "operating thetan" levels. Details about what happens in these advanced stages remain closely guarded Scientology secrets, but at the very end of the process, thetans are supposed to gain power over the physical world; consequently, according to founder L. Ron Hubbard, they "feel no need of bodies," ending the cycle of birth and death and becoming pure, incorporeal souls.[78]

78. Rastogi, "Scientologist: Isaac Hayes' Soul?"

Appendix C

Lists of Prohibited
Behaviors and Commandments

of Major Religions with a Final Judgment,
plus Hinduism and Buddhism

Christianity: The Ten Commandments[1]

1. Thou shalt have no other gods before me

2. Thou shalt not make unto thee any graven image

3. Thou shalt not take the name of the LORD thy God in vain

4. Remember the sabbath day, to keep it holy

5. Honour thy father and thy mother

6. Thou shalt not murder

7. Thou shalt not commit adultery

8. Thou shalt not steal

9. Thou shalt not bear false witness against thy neighbor

10. Thou shalt not covet

1. *Wikipedia*, s.v. "Ten Commandments."

Christianity: Seven Deadly Sins[2]

1. Pride
2. Greed
3. Wrath
4. Envy
5. Lust
6. Gluttony
7. Sloth/Laziness

Christianity: Seven Detestable Sins (Proverbs 6:16 NIV)

1. Haughty eyes
2. A lying tongue
3. Hands that shed innocent blood
4. A heart that devises wicked schemes
5. Feet that are quick to rush into evil
6. A false witness who pours out lies
7. A man who stirs up dissension among brothers

Christianity: Sins That Cry to Heaven[3]

1. Homicide, abortion, infanticide, fratricide, patricide, and matricide
2. Non-procreative sexual acts (sodomy)
3. Oppression of the poor
4. Taking advantage of and defrauding workers

2. *Wikipedia*, s.v. "Seven Deadly Sins."
3. *Wikipedia*, s.v. "Sins Cry to Heaven."

Islam: Some of the Major Sins
(potentially up to 70 in total)[4]

1. Shirk (associating anything with Allah)

2. Despair of Allah's mercy

3. Disobeying parents

4. Zina (adultery)

5. Sodomy

6. Theft

7. Consumption of alcohol / other intoxicants

8. Gambling

9. Backbiting (saying bad things about a person who is not there)

10. Leaving daily prayer (Salah)

11. Zakat evasion

12. Witchcraft

13. Killing one whom Allah has declared inviolate without a just case

14. Consuming the property of an orphan

15. Devouring usury

16. Turning back when the army advances

17. False accusation of chaste women who are believers but indiscreet

Hinduism: The Five Mortal Sins—Mahā Pātakas[5]

1. *brahma-hatya*—killing a (learned) Brahmaṇa

2. *sura-pānam*—drinking Sura (alcohol)

3. *suvarṇa-steya*—stealing gold

4. *guru-talpaga*—adultery with a Guru's wife

5. *saṃsargas taiḥ*—associating with these offenders

4. *Wikipedia*, s.v. "Islamic Views on Sin."
5. Sivan, "Five Mortal Sins."

Hinduism: The Ten Venial Sins[6]

1. Thinking harmful thoughts directed toward others
2. Clinging to irrational and erroneous views and doctrines
3. Lying
4. Slandering
5. Gossiping
6. Abusing others
7. Giving false advice or teachings
8. Causing physical injury to other living beings
9. Sexual misconduct
10. Not rendering assistance in time of need

Buddhism: Anantarika-karma in Theravada Buddhism Is a Heinous Crime[7]

1. Injuring a Buddha
2. Killing an Arhat
3. Creating schism in the society of Sangha
4. Matricide
5. Patricide

Primal-Indigenous (see Christianity and Islam)

---

6. Sivan, "Ten Venial Sins."

7. *Wikipedia*, s.v. "Buddhist Views on Sin."

Appendix C

African Traditional: Forbidden Criminal Actions[8]

1. Adultery
2. Breach of Covenant
3. Burglary
4. Fornication
5. Incest
6. Kidnapping
7. Irreverence and unkindness to parents
8. Lying
9. Murder
10. Rape
11. Seduction
12. Speaking evil of rulers
13. Swearing falsely
14. Theft
15. Sodomy
16. Malice

Judaism: First 50 of 613 Commandments from the Hebrew Bible as enumerated by Maimonides[9]

1. To know there is a God—Exod 20:2
2. Not to even think that there are other gods besides Him—Standard: Exod 20:3; Yemenite: Exod 20:2
3. To know that God is One—Deut 6:4
4. To love God—Deut 6:5
5. To fear God—Deut 10:20

8. Adewale, "Crime and African Religion."
9. *Wikipedia*, s.v. "613 Commandments."

6. To sanctify God's Name—Lev 22:32

7. Not to profane God's Name—Lev 22:32

8. Not to destroy objects associated with God's Name—Deut 12:4

9. To listen to the prophet speaking in God's Name—Deut 18:15

10. Not to try the LORD unduly—Deut 6:16

11. To emulate God's ways—Deut 28:9

12. To cleave to those who know God—Deut 10:20

13. To love other Jews—Lev 19:18

14. To love converts—Deut 10:19

15. Not to hate fellow Jews—Lev 19:17

16. To reprove a sinner—Lev 19:17

17. Not to embarrass others—Lev 19:17

18. Not to oppress the weak—Exod 22:21

19. Not to speak derogatorily of others—Lev 19:16

20. Not to take revenge—Lev 19:18

21. Not to bear a grudge—Lev 19:18

22. To learn Torah—Deut 6:7

23. To honor those who teach and know Torah—Lev 19:32

24. Not to inquire into idolatry—Lev 19:4

25. Not to follow the whims of your heart or what your eyes see—Num 15:39

26. Not to blaspheme—Exod 22:27

27. Not to worship idols in the manner they are worshiped—Standard: Exod 20:6; Yemenite: Exod 20:5

28. Not to worship idols in the four ways we worship God—Standard: Exod 20:6; Yemenite: Exod 20:5

29. Not to make an idol for yourself—Standard: Exod 20:5; Yemenite: Exod 20:4

30. Not to make an idol for others—Lev 19:4

31. Not to make human forms even for decorative purposes—Standard: Exod 20:21; Yemenite: Exod 20:20

32. Not to turn a city to idolatry—Deut 13:14

33. To burn a city that has turned to idol worship—Deut 13:17

34. Not to rebuild it as a city—Deut 13:17

35. Not to derive benefit from it—Deut 13:18

36. Not to missionize an individual to idol worship—Deut 13:12

37. Not to love the idolater—Deut 13:9

38. Not to cease hating the idolater—Deut 13:9

39. Not to save the idolater—Deut 13:9

40. Not to say anything in the idolater's defense—Deut 13:9

41. Not to refrain from incriminating the idolater—Deut 13:9

42. Not to prophesy in the name of idolatry—Deut 13:14

43. Not to listen to a false prophet—Deut 13:4

44. Not to prophesy falsely in the name of God—Deut 18:20

45. Not to be afraid of the false prophet—Deut 18:22

46. Not to swear in the name of an idol—Exod 23:13

47. Not to perform ov (medium)—Lev 19:31

48. Not to perform yidoni ("magical seer")—Lev 19:31

49. Not to pass your children through the fire to Molech—Lev 18:21

50. Not to erect a pillar in a public place of worship—Deut 16:22

Bahá'í: Laws and Ordinances (Partial List)[10]

1. Pray daily

2. Observe annual 19-day fast

3. Marriage recommended but not obligatory

4. Create a will

10. *Wikipedia*, s.v. "Bahá'í Laws," 5. Laws and Ordinances.

5. Backbiting and gossip are prohibited

6. Drinking alcohol or taking drugs are forbidden, except by a doctor's orders

7. Comply with Huqúqu'lláh, the "Right of God" (Tithing)

Bahá'í: Prohibitions (Partial List)[11]

1. Believing personal interpretations of the Bahá'í writings as authoritative

2. Slavery

3. Asceticism

4. Monasticism

5. Begging

6. Clergy

7. Use of Pulpits

8. The kissing of hands (as a form of obeisance)

9. Confession of sins

10. Gambling

11. Homosexual acts

12. Cruelty to animals

13. Sloth

14. Calumny

15. The carrying of arms unless essential

16. Assault

17. Shaving of one's head

18. Adultery and sexual intercourse between unmarried couples

19. Arson

20. Murder

21. Theft

---

11. *Wikipedia*, s.v. "Bahá'í Laws," 5.9. Other Prohibitions.

Zoroastrianism: In the Menog-i-khard (chapter 36) we find the following list of 30 grievous sins[12]

1. Of the sin which people commit, unnatural intercourse is the most heinous.

2. The second is he who has suffered or performed intercourse with men.

3. The third, who slays a righteous man.

4. The fourth, who breaks off a next-of-kin marriage.

5. The fifth, who destroys the arrangement of an adopted son (sator).

6. The sixth, who smites the fire of Warharan.

7. The seventh, who kills a water-beaver.

8. The eighth, who worships an idol.

9. The ninth, who believes and wishes to worship in every religion.

10. The tenth, who consumes anything which is received into his custody, and becomes an embezzler.

11. The eleventh is he who, through sinfulness, provides support for wickedness.

12. The twelfth, who does no work, but eats unthankfully and unlawfully.

13. The thirteenth, who commits heresy (zandikih).

14. The fourteenth, who commits witchcraft.

15. The fifteenth, who commits apostasy (aharmokih).

16. The sixteenth, who commits demon-worship.

17. The seventeenth, who commits theft, or abetting (avagitih) of thieves.

18. The eighteenth, who commits promise-breaking.

19. The nineteenth, who commits maliciousness.

20. The twentieth, who commits oppression to make the things of others his own.

21. The twenty-first, who distresses a righteous man.

22. The twenty-second, who commits slander.

23. The twenty-third, who commits arrogance.

12. Jayaram V, "Zoroastrianism: Sins in Menog-i-khard."

24. The twenty-fourth, who goes to a professional courtesan.

25. The twenty-fifth, who commits ingratitude.

26. The twenty-sixth, who speaks false and untrue.

27. The twenty-seventh, who causes discontent as to the affairs of those who are departed.

28. The twenty-eighth, whose pleasure is from viciousness and harassing the good.

29. The twenty-ninth, who considers sin as to be urged on, and a good work as a day's delay.

30. And the thirtieth, who becomes grieved by that happiness which is provided by him for anyone.

Zoroastrianism: List of Sins in Denkard[13]

1. Contempt for the religion, speaking ill of it, disobeying the dictates thereof, and self willedness,

2. thinking of matters pertaining to a wicked religion, accepting anything from those professing a wicked religion,

3. not fighting with the Devs and the wicked persons,

4. becoming related to unbelievers by giving them children in marriage,

5. not giving good help to other people in the virtuous pursuit of their callings in the world,

6. disloyalty to partners,

7. sordidness,

8. doing wrongful acts,

9. harboring enmity towards the good people who constantly invoke God,

10. pleasing the wicked; also, worshipping the Devil,

11. doing harm to pious men,

12. impairing (their) sanctity,

13. omitting [sic; read: committing] sodomy,

13. Jayaram V, "Zoroastrianism: Sins in Denkard."

14. practicing sorcery,

15. highway robbery,

16. committing adultery,

17. decreasing the progeny, (i.e., not caring to increase one's progeny by timely marriage), and impairing the other Dominion (i.e., that pertaining to the next world),

18. doing injustice,

19. false teaching,

20. depriving the adopted son or the heir of his rights,

21. depriving a family of its guardian,

22. loving the wicked,

23. giving false evidence,

24. helping the untruthful,

25. also putting out the Atash Behram Warharan fire,

26. eating of putrefying animal matter,

27. throwing the same into fire or water,

28. burying the dead under the ground against the law (of the religion), not within the distance prescribed by the religion), and single-handed, which is a sin deserving of death.

Zoroastrianism: Other Capital Offences[14]

1. killing the water-dog and other species of dogs,

2. prostitution,

3. sexual intercourse with women during menstruation,

4. Avarun Marzi (i.e., unnatural intercourse with a woman),

5. drunkenness,

6. theft,

7. oppression,

14. Jayaram V, "Zoroastrianism: Capital Offences."

8. sordidness,

9. back-biting,

10. deception,

11. doing dirty acts,

12. eating or drinking without the Vaj (i.e., saying grace),

13. moving about without the Sudre and the Kusti (the sacred shirt and girdle),

14. making water in a standing posture,

15. obscene speech,

16. doing every sort of immoral deeds,

17. and other such acts.

Unitarian Universalism
(see Christianity, Islam, and Judaism)

Rastafarianism: All Rastas[15]

One should abstain from, avoid, or not do:

1. Animal products and by-products

2. Processed foods and genetically modified foods

3. Sodium salt

4. Seafoods that are scavengers

5. The use of alcoholic beverages (all forms of beer, stouts, and wines)

6. The use and sale of drugs (Legal or Illegal)

7. Using the methods of justice of the State, except in extreme situations where State law is appropriate to dictate the outcome of the situation

8. Using methods of vigilante justice or any action that would endanger or threaten the security of the Rastafari family

15. "Rastafari Code of Conduct," pp. 14–20, http://rastaites.com/download/livity/ Rastafari_Code_of_Conduct.pdf.

9. Homosexuality

10. Sodomy

11. Sex with children or animals

12. Rape

13. Oral Sex

14. Prostitution

15. Whoredom

16. Entering in to a relationship knowingly aware that a person is already in an intimate situation with another

17. Entering in to a sexual or intimate relationship that may cause disharmony, grief or strife

18. Entering in to a sexual or intimate relationship involving multiple partners

19. Displaying any activity in public that depicts sexual intent

20. Abuse, slander, carry tales, hearsay, or disgrace any Rastafari brethren, sistren, house, mansion, organization, or others, in public places, through Printed Press, Radio, Television, Internet, or any other communication media

Rastafarianism: Rastafari Reggae Musicians, Singers, Promoters, MCs and DJs[16]

One should refrain from:

1. Using the names of Qadamawi Haile Selassie and Empress Menen casually or in vain while on or off stage

2. Creating music and dance that trivializes a woman's sexuality or tramples on her I-tegrity or self-worth, or influences ones to consider or commit acts of violence against her

3. Creating music and lyrics that influence anyone to commit crimes against another

4. Promoting music videos with lewd, sexually explicit or immoral behavior

16. "Rastafari Code of Conduct," 18.

Appendix D

Religious Affiliation
of Inmates in US Prisons

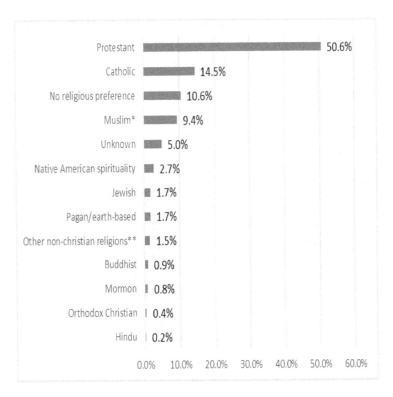

Protestant — 50.6%
Catholic — 14.5%
No religious preference — 10.6%
Muslim* — 9.4%
Unknown — 5.0%
Native American spirituality — 2.7%
Jewish — 1.7%
Pagan/earth-based — 1.7%
Other non-christian religions** — 1.5%
Buddhist — 0.9%
Mormon — 0.8%
Orthodox Christian — 0.4%
Hindu — 0.2%

0.0% 10.0% 20.0% 30.0% 40.0% 50.0% 60.0%

**Mean religious affiliation of inmates in US prisons,
as reported by prison chaplains in 2011[1]**

1. Statista, "Inmates in U.S. Prisons."

Appendix D

THIS STATISTIC SHOWS US prison chaplains estimations of the percentage of inmates belonging to different organized faiths and religions as of 2011. Chaplains surveyed reported that on average 50.6 percent of inmates were of protestant faiths.

Additional Information on Religion in United States Prisons

The religious affiliation of inmates in the United States, the country with the most prisoners per head globally, is reasonably similar to the religious affiliations of the society overall. That said, the proportion of nonreligious inmates and those declining to express their religious affiliation is smaller than the overall proportion. In contrast the number of Muslim inmates is disproportionately large in comparison with wider society. As a result a sizable share of prison chaplains identity [sic; read: *identify*] as Muslim, catering to the preferences of the Muslim prison population.

Following the September 11, 2001, World Trade Center attacks and the subsequent War on Terror launched by George W. Bush, religious extremism has been a target of public debate and policy. The debate has stretched into prisons particularly with the United States prison on Guantanamo Bay holding a number of suspected terrorists related to religious extremism. In turn, fears have been raised that prisons have become a hotbed for religious extremism.

Critics have argued that religious extremism has provided an unwarranted justification for the conviction of Muslims. Regardless of the supposed reason for their imprisonment, this disproportionate number presents a problem for United States policy makers.

Religious Affiliation of Inmates in US Prisons

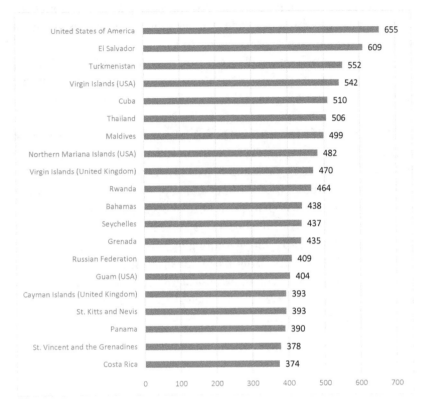

United States of America	655
El Salvador	609
Turkmenistan	552
Virgin Islands (USA)	542
Cuba	510
Thailand	506
Maldives	499
Northern Mariana Islands (USA)	482
Virgin Islands (United Kingdom)	470
Rwanda	464
Bahamas	438
Seychelles	437
Grenada	435
Russian Federation	409
Guam (USA)	404
Cayman Islands (United Kingdom)	393
St. Kitts and Nevis	393
Panama	390
St. Vincent and the Grenadines	378
Costa Rica	374

**Countries with the largest number of prisoners
per 100,000 of the national population, as of July 2018[2]**

This statistic represents the countries with the most prisoners per 100,000 inhabitants, as of July 19, 2018. The United States had the highest prisoner rate, with 655 prisoners per 100,000 of the national population.

Prisoners in the United States

As the statistic above illustrates, the United States has one of the highest rates of incarceration in the world. With 655 inmates per 100 thousand of population, the United States is by far the leader among large industrialized nations in incarceration. Russia comes closest at 451, though there is no data regarding China's incarceration rate available.

2. Statista, "Countries with Largest Number of Prisoners."

Appendix D

Not only is the United States among the leading countries worldwide in incarcerations per 100 thousand of population, but it was also home to the largest total number of prisoners in 2014.

Roughly 2.2 million people were incarcerated in the United States in 2014. China's estimated prison population totaled to 1.7 million people that year. Other nations with population sizes comparable to the United States have far fewer prisoners.

The majority of US prisoners in federal correctional facilities were of black or African American origin. As of 2011, there were about half a million male and about 26 thousand female black, non-Hispanic prisoners. They made up 40 percent of all incarcerated persons in the United States but accounted for only 13 percent of the total US population.

About 237 thousand prisoners in state facilities were sentenced for drug-related offenses, accounting for roughly 17.4 percent of all state prisoners in the United States. Drug-related offenses, such as trafficking and possession, were the most common cause of imprisonment in state prisons. Second most common were felonies, such as robbery and murder, at 13.6 and 12.2 percent, respectively.

Appendix E

Probability of a Good Afterlife

for each Major Religion

Afterlife possibility	Entity determining the outcome	Outcome	Religion with unique or additional requirement	Christianity	Islam	Nonreligious	Hinduism
No Soul							
				1.00	1.00	1.00	1.00
Mortal Soul							
				1.00	1.00	1.00	1.00
Without a Trace							
				1.00	1.00	1.00	1.00
Déjà Vu							
	Individual			0.50	0.50	0.50	0.50
The Merry-Go-Round							

Appendix E

Afterlife possibility	Entity determining the outcome	Outcome	Religion with unique or additional requirement	Christianity	Islam	Nonreligious	Hinduism
Ain't No Stopping Us Now		No Escape		1.00	1.00	1.00	1.00
Reunited, and It Feels So Good	Individual	Reunion		1.00	1.00	1.00	1.00
Eraser	God/ Individual	Reunion/ Destroyed		1.00	1.00	1.00	1.00
Judgment Day							
Control	Individual	Close to God		0.50	0.50	0.50	0.50
The Scales of Justice	God						
Purified		Purified		1.00	1.00	0.00	1.00
Destroyed		Destroyed		1.00	1.00	0.00	1.00
Punished		Heaven					
			Islam	0.00	0.50	0.00	0.00
			African Traditional & Diasporic	0.50	0.50	0.00	0.50
			Judaism	0.50	0.50	0.00	0.50

Probability of a Good Afterlife

Afterlife possibility	Entity determining the outcome	Outcome	Religion with unique or additional requirement	Christianity	Islam	Nonreligious	Hinduism
The Lion and the Lamb	Jesus Christ	Christianity		1.00	0.00	0.00	0.00
Decision Day							
	Individual			1.00	1.00	1.00	1.00
Extreme Measures							
Good Place				1.00	1.00	1.00	1.00
Bad Place				0.00	0.00	0.00	0.00
Overall Probability				0.7647	0.7353	0.5294	0.7059

Appendix E

Afterlife Possibility	Entity determining the outcome	Outcome	Religion with unique or additional requirement	Chinese Traditional			Buddhism
				Taoism	Confucianism	Folk-Religionist	
No Soul							
				1.00	1.00	1.00	1.00
Mortal Soul							
				1.00	1.00	1.00	1.00
Without a Trace							
				1.00	1.00	1.00	1.00
Déjà Vu							
	Individual			0.50	0.50	0.50	0.50
The Merry-Go-Round							
Ain't No Stopping Us Now		No Escape		1.00	1.00	1.00	1.00
Reunited, and It Feels So Good	Individual	Reunion		1.00	1.00	1.00	1.00
Eraser	God/ Individual	Reunion/ Destroyed		1.00	1.00	1.00	1.00
Judgment Day							

Probability of a Good Afterlife

Afterlife Possibility	Entity determining the outcome	Outcome	Religion with unique or additional requirement	Chinese Traditional			Buddhism
				Taoism	Confucianism	Folk-Religionist	
Control	Individual	Close to God		0.50	0.50	0.50	0.50
The Scales of Justice	God						
Purified		Purified		0.00	0.00	1.00	0.00
Destroyed		Destroyed		0.00	0.00	1.00	0.00
Punished		Heaven					
			Islam	0.00	0.00	0.00	0.00
			African Traditional & Diasporic	0.00	0.00	0.50	0.00
			Judaism	0.00	0.00	0.50	0.00
The Lion and the Lamb	Jesus Christ		Christianity	0.00	0.00	0.00	0.00
Decision Day							
	Individual			1.00	1.00	1.00	1.00
Extreme Measures							

Appendix E

Afterlife Possibility	Entity determining the outcome	Outcome	Religion with unique or additional requirement	Chinese Traditional			Buddhism
				Taoism	Confucianism	Folk-Religionist	
Good Place				1.00	1.00	1.00	1.00
Bad Place				0.00	0.00	0.00	0.00
Overall Probability				0.5294	0.5294	0.7059	0.5294

Probability of a Good Afterlife

| Afterlife Possibility | Entity determining the outcome | Outcome | Religion with unique or additional requirement | Primal-Indigenous | | | | |
| | | | | Ethno-religionist | | | Animist | Shamanist |
				Christianity based	Islam based	Buddhism based		
No Soul				1.00	1.00	1.00	1.00	1.00
Mortal Soul				1.00	1.00	1.00	1.00	1.00
Without a Trace				1.00	1.00	1.00	1.00	1.00
Déjà Vu	Individual			0.50	0.50	0.50	0.50	0.50
The Merry-Go-Round								
Ain't No Stopping Us Now		No Escape		1.00	1.00	1.00	1.00	1.00
Reunited, and It Feels So Good	Individual	Reunion		1.00	1.00	1.00	1.00	1.00
Eraser	God/Individual	Reunion/Destroyed		1.00	1.00	1.00	1.00	1.00

Afterlife Possibility	Entity determining the outcome	Outcome	Religion with unique or additional requirement	Primal-Indigenous				
				Ethno-religionist			Animist	Shamanist
				Christianity based	Islam based	Buddhism based		
Judgment Day								
Control	Individual	Close to God		0.50	0.50	0.50	0.50	0.50
The Scales of Justice	God							
Purified		Purified		1.00	1.00	0.00	0.00	0.00
Destroyed		Destroyed		1.00	1.00	0.00	0.00	0.00
Punished		Heaven						
			Islam	0.00	0.50	0.00	0.00	0.00
			African Traditional & Diasporic	0.50	0.50	0.00	0.00	0.00
			Judaism	0.50	0.50	0.00	0.00	0.00
The Lion and the Lamb	Jesus Christ		Christianity	1.00	0.00	0.00	0.00	0.00
Decision Day								
	Individual			1.00	1.00	1.00	1.00	1.00

Probability of a Good Afterlife

Afterlife Possibility	Entity determining the outcome	Outcome	Religion with unique or additional requirement	Primal-Indigenous				
				Ethno-religionist			Animist	Shamanist
				Christianity based	Islam based	Buddhism based		
xtreme easures								
ood ace				1.00	1.00	1.00	1.00	1.00
d Place				0.00	0.00	0.00	0.00	0.00
verall obability				0.7647	0.7353	0.5294	0.5294	0.5294

Afterlife possibility	Entity determining the outcome	Outcome	Religion with unique or additional requirement	African Traditional & Diasporic*	Sikhism	Juche	Spiritism	Judaism
No Soul				1.00	1.00	1.00	1.00	1.00
Mortal Soul				1.00	1.00	1.00	1.00	1.00
Without a Trace				1.00	1.00	1.00	1.00	1.00
Déjà Vu	Individual			0.50	0.50	0.50	0.50	0.50
The Merry-Go-Round								
Ain't No Stopping Us Now		No Escape		1.00	1.00	1.00	1.00	1.00
Reunited, and It Feels So Good	Individual	Reunion		1.00	1.00	1.00	1.00	1.00
Eraser	God/Individual	Reunion/Destroyed		1.00	1.00	1.00	1.00	1.00

Probability of a Good Afterlife

Afterlife possibility	Entity determining the outcome	Outcome	Religion with unique or additional requirement	African Traditional & Diasporic*	Sikhism	Juche	Spiritism	Judaism
Judgment Day								
Control	Individual	Close to God		0.50	0.50	0.50	0.50	0.50
The Scales of Justice	God							
Purified		Purified		1.00	1.00	0.00	1.00	1.00
Destroyed		Destroyed		1.00	1.00	0.00	1.00	1.00
Punished		Heaven						
			Islam	0.00	0.50	0.00	0.50	0.50
			African Traditional & Diasporic	0.50	0.50	0.00	0.50	0.50
			Judaism	0.50	0.50	0.00	0.50	0.50
The Lion and the Lamb	Jesus Christ		Christianity	0.00	0.00	0.00	0.00	0.00
Decision Day								
	Individual			1.00	1.00	1.00	1.00	1.00

Appendix E

	Afterlife possibility	Entity determining the outcome	Outcome	Religion with unique or additional requirement	African Traditional & Diasporic*	Sikhism	Juche	Spiritism	Judaism
Extreme Measures									
Good Place					1.00	1.00	1.00	1.00	1.00
Bad Place					0.00	0.00	0.00	0.00	0.00
Overall Probability					0.7059	0.7353	0.5294	0.7353	0.7353

*Note: Scoring for those groups within the religion that ascribe to a final judgment with the possibility of eternal punishment. Other afterlife possibilities include no heaven and no hell (scored under Déjà Vu) and endless reincarnation (scored under The Merry-Go-Round: Ain't No Stopping Us Now).

Probability of a Good Afterlife

Afterlife Possibility	Entity determining the outcome	Outcome	Religion with unique or additional requirement	Baháʼí	Jainism	Shinto	Cao Dai	Zoroastrianism
No Soul								
				1.00	1.00	1.00	1.00	1.00
Mortal Soul								
				1.00	1.00	1.00	1.00	1.00
Without a Trace								
				1.00	1.00	1.00	1.00	1.00
Déjà Vu								
	Individual			0.50	0.50	0.50	0.50	0.50
The Merry-Go-Round								
Ain't No Stopping Us Now		No Escape		1.00	1.00	1.00	1.00	1.00
Reunited, and It Feels So Good	Individual	Reunion		1.00	1.00	1.00	1.00	1.00
Eraser	God/Individual	Reunion/Destroyed		1.00	1.00	1.00	1.00	1.00

Appendix E

Afterlife Possibility	Entity determining the outcome	Outcome	Religion with unique or additional requirement	Bahá'í	Jainism	Shinto	Cao Dai	Zoroastrianism
Judgment Day								
Control	Individual	Close to God		0.50	0.50	0.50	0.50	0.50
The Scales of Justice	God							
Purified		Purified		1.00	0.00	0.00	1.00	1.00
Destroyed		Destroyed		1.00	0.00	0.00	1.00	1.00
Punished		Heaven						
			Islam	0.50	0.00	0.00	0.00	0.50
			African Traditional & Diasporic	0.50	0.00	0.00	0.50	0.50
			Judaism	0.50	0.00	0.00	0.50	0.50
The Lion and the Lamb	Jesus Christ		Christianity	0.00	0.00	0.00	0.00	0.00
Decision Day								
	Individual			1.00	1.00	1.00	1.00	1.00

Probability of a Good Afterlife

Afterlife Possibility	Entity determining the outcome	Outcome	Religion with unique or additional requirement	Bahá'í	Jainism	Shinto	Cao Dai	Zoroastrianism
Extreme Measures								
Good Place				1.00	1.00	1.00	1.00	1.00
Bad Place				0.00	0.00	0.00	0.00	0.00
Overall Probability				0.7353	0.5294	0.5294	0.7059	0.7353

Appendix E

Afterlife possibility	Entity determining the outcome	Outcome	Religion with unique or additional requirement	Tenrikyo	Neopaganism	Unitarian Universalism**	Rastafarianism	Scientology
No Soul				1.00	1.00	1.00	1.00	1.00
Mortal Soul				1.00	1.00	1.00	1.00	1.00
Without a Trace				1.00	1.00	1.00	1.00	1.00
Déjà Vu	Individual			0.50	0.50	0.50	0.50	0.50
The Merry-Go-Round								
Ain't No Stopping Us Now		No Escape		1.00	1.00	1.00	1.00	1.00
Reunited, and It Feels So Good	Individual	Reunion		1.00	1.00	1.00	1.00	1.00
Eraser	God/Individual	Reunion/ Destroyed		1.00	1.00	1.00	1.00	1.00

Probability of a Good Afterlife

Afterlife possibility	Entity determining the outcome	Outcome	Religion with unique or additional requirement	Tenrikyo	Neopaganism	Unitarian Universalism**	Rastafarianism	Scientology
Judgment Day								
Control	Individual	Close to God		0.50	0.50	0.50	0.50	0.50
The Scales of Justice	God							
Purified		Purified		1.00	0.00	1.00	1.00	1.00
Destroyed		Destroyed		1.00	0.00	1.00	1.00	1.00
Punished		Heaven						
			Islam	0.50	0.00	0.50	0.50	0.50
			African Traditional & Diasporic	0.50	0.00	0.50	0.50	0.50
			Judaism	0.50	0.00	0.50	0.50	0.50
The Lion and the Lamb	Jesus Christ		Christianity	0.00	0.00	0.00	0.00	0.00
Decision Day								
	Individual			1.00	1.00	1.00	1.00	1.00

Appendix E

	Afterlife possibility	Entity determining the outcome	Outcome	Religion with unique or additional requirement	Tenrikyo	Neopaganism	Unitarian Universalism**	Rastafarianism	Scientology
Extreme Measures									
Good Place					1.00	1.00	1.00	1.00	1.00
Bad Place					0.00	0.00	0.00	0.00	0.00
Overall Probability					0.7353	0.5294	0.7353	0.7353	0.7353

**Note: Scoring for traditional Unitarian Universalists who accept the doctrine of universal reconciliation. Adherents who have adopted the beliefs of other faiths would receive the scores of those specific religions.

Bibliography

Abbott, Karen. "The Fox Sisters and the Rap on Spiritualism." *Smithsonian* magazine, October 30, 2012. https://www.smithsonianmag.com/history/the-fox-sisters-and-the-rap-on-spiritualism-99663697/.

Adewale, S. A. "Crime and African Traditional Religion." http://www.africaspeaks.com/reasoning/index.php?topic=2978.0;wap2.

BBC. "Religions: Beliefs: Beliefs." http://www.bbc.co.uk/religion/religions/spiritualism/beliefs/beliefs_1.shtml.

———. "Religions: Beliefs; Declaration of Principles." http://www.bbc.co.uk/religion/religions/spiritualism/beliefs/beliefs_1.shtml.

———. "Religions: The Soul; Jain Beliefs about the Soul." http://www.bbc.co.uk/religion/religions/jainism/beliefs/soul.shtml.

Beliefnet. "What Neo-Pagans Believe: Central Tenets of Neo-Paganism, Based on the Questions in the Belief-O-Matic Quiz." https://www.beliefnet.com/faiths/2001/06/what-neo-pagans-believe.aspx.

Bullock, Olivia. "What Happens When You Die? A Look at Different Chinese Mythologies on Death and the Afterlife: According to Traditional Chinese Mythology/Folk Religions." *The World of Chinese* (website), October 21, 2014. https://www.theworldofchinese.com/2014/10/what-happens-when-you-die/.

Camps, Marc Arenas. "How Many Species Live on Earth?" *All You Need Is Biology* (website), May 20, 2018. https://allyouneedisbiology.wordpress.com/2018/05/20/biodiversity-species/.

Cline, Austin. "What Is Secular Humanism?" *Learn Religions* (website). Last updated April 26, 2019. https://www.learnreligions.com/religious-vs-secular-humanism-248117.

Denosky, J. "Spiritualism and Spiritual Travel: A Spiritualist's View of After-Death States." http://www.spiritualtravel.org/OBE/spiritualist.html.

Dr. Jeff. "How Many NDEs Occur in the United States Every Day?" https://www.nderf.org/NDERF/Research/number_nde_usa.htm.

The Editors of Encyclopaedia Britannica. "Multiple Souls." *Britannica.com*. https://www.britannica.com/topic/multiple-souls.

———. "Tenrikyō." *Britannica.com*. https://www.britannica.com/topic/Tenrikyo.

Gardiner, Eileen. "About Zoroastrian Hell: Elements of Zoroastrian Afterlife." *Hell-on-Line* (website). http://www.hell-on-line.org/AboutZOR.html.

Hafiz, Yasmine. "Yazidi Religious Beliefs: History, Facts and Traditions of Iraq's Persecuted Minority; Beliefs and Cosmology." *HuffPost*, August 13, 2014. https://www.huffpost.com/entry/yazidi-religious-beliefs_n_5671903.

Bibliography

Hathaway, Bill. "Scientists Restore Some Functions in a Pig's Brain Hours after Death." *YaleNews*, April 17, 2019. https://news.yale.edu/2019/04/17/scientists-restore-some-functions-pigs-brain-hours-after-death?utm_source=YNemail&utm_medium=email&utm_campaign=yn-04-18-19.

Horton, Sarah J. "Shinto." *Encyclopedia of Death and Dying* (website). http://www.deathreference.com/Sh-Sy/Shinto.html.

Hosseini, Seyedeh Behnaz. "Life after Death in Manichaeism and Yārsān: Conclusion." http://www.yaresan.com/about-yaresan/articles/424-life-after-death-in-manichaeism-and-yarsan.

Jayaram V. "Zoroastrianism: Types of Sins and Expiation of Sin; Capital Offences." https://www.hinduwebsite.com/zoroastrianism/sin.asp.

———. "Zoroastrianism: Types of Sins and Expiation of Sin; List of Sins in Denkard." https://www.hinduwebsite.com/zoroastrianism/sin.asp.

———. "Zoroastrianism: Types of Sin and Expiation of Sin: List of Sins in the Menog-i-khard." https://www.hinduwebsite.com/zoroastrianism/sin.asp.

Khalsa, Sukhmandir. "Sikhism and the Afterlife." http://sikhism.about.com/od/sikhism101/qt/Sikh_Afterlife.htm.

Lewis, James R. *Encyclopedia of Afterlife Beliefs and Phenomena*. Detroit: Gale Research, 1994.

Long, Jody, and Jeffrey Long. "Dr. George Rodonaia." https://www.nderf.org/Experiences/1george_rodonaia_nde.html.

New World Encyclopedia. "Animism." https://www.newworldencyclopedia.org/entry/animism.

Patheos Religion Library. "Baha'i." Patheos Religion Library. https://www.patheos.com/library/bahai.

———. "Buddhism." Patheos Religion Library. https://www.patheos.com/library/buddhism.

———. "Christianity." Patheos Religion Library. http://www.patheos.com/Library/Christianity.

———. "Confucianism." Patheos Religion Library. http://www.patheos.com/Library/Confucianism.

———. "Hinduism." Patheos Religion Library. http://www.patheos.com/Library/Hinduism.

———. "Islam." Patheos Religion Library. http://www.patheos.com/Library/Islam.

———. "Juche." Patheos Religion Library. http://www.patheos.com/Library/Juche.html.

———. "Judaism." Patheos Religion Library. http://www.patheos.com/Library/Judaism.

———. "Shinto." Patheos Religion Library. http://www.patheos.com/Library/Shinto.

———. "Taoism: Beliefs; Afterlife and Salvation." Patheos Religion Library. http://www.patheos.com/Library/Taoism.

———. "Unitarian-Universalism." Patheos Religion Library. http://www.patheos.com/Library/Unitarian-Universalism.

"The Rastafari Code of Conduct." Available online at http://rastaites.com/download/livity/Rastafari_Code_of_Conduct.pdf.

Rastogi, Nina Shen. "The Afterlife for Scientologists: What Will Happen to Isaac Hayes' Legendary Soul?" *Slate*, August 11, 2008. https://slate.com/news-and-politics/2008/08/where-do-scientologists-go-when-they-die.html.

Bibliography

Rooke, Andrew. "Reincarnation in African Traditional Religion." From *Sunrise* magazine, November 1980. http://www.theosophy-nw.org/theosnw/world/africa/af-rook2. htm.

Rose, Rabbi Or N. "Heaven and Hell in Jewish Tradition." https://www.myjewishlearning. com/article/heaven-and-hell-in-jewish-tradition/.

Sivan, Rami. "What Are All the Sins in Hinduism? The Five Mortal Sins: Mahā Pātakas." https://www.quora.com/What-are-all-the-sins-of-Hinduism.

———. "What Are All the Sins in Hinduism? The Ten Venial Sins." https://www.quora. com/What-are-all-the-sins-of-Hinduism.

Statista. "Countries with the Largest Number of Prisoners per 100,000 of the National Population, as of July 2018." https://www.statista.com/statistics/445707/countries-with-the-highest-prison-occupancy-level/.

———. "Religious Affiliation of Inmates in U.S. Prisons, 2011." https://www.statista.com/ statistics/234653/religious-affiliation-of-us-prisoners/.

Stuart, James. "Beliefs of the Zoroastrians on Hell: Hell." https://classroom.synonym.com/ beliefs-of-the-zoroastrians-on-hell-12085986.html.

Unitarian Universalist Association. "Leader Resource 3: Common Views among Universalists; Afterlife." https://www.uua.org/re/tapestry/adults/newuu/ workshop1/160230.shtml.

US Department of Justice. "Proof of Innocence: Inmate Ronald Cotton's Story." US Department of Justice, Office of Justice Programs, Office for Victims of Crime. https:// ovc.ojp.gov/sites/g/files/xyckuh226/files/publications/bulletins/dna_4_2001/ dna11_4_01.html.

Van Wyk, I. W. C. "The Final Judgment in African Perspectives: The Absence of the Notion of Judgment in Africa; African Traditional Religion." https://repository.up.ac.za/ bitstream/handle/2263/14961/VanWyk_Final%282006%29.pdf?sequence=1.

Wallner, Chris. "Get Blown Away by This List of the 7 Windiest Places on Earth." https:// snowbrains.com/get-blown-away-by-this-list-of-the-7-windiest-places-on-earth/.

Zammit, Victor J. "How Different Religions View the Afterlife: Judaism." http://www. victorzammit.com/articles/religions3.html.

———. "How Different Religions View the Afterlife: Spiritualism/Spiritism." http://www. victorzammit.com/articles/religions3.html.

CPSIA information can be obtained
at www.ICGtesting.com
Printed in the USA
BVHW040905030621
608548BV00013B/1081